Changeformational™
Change Happens &
Transformations Occur ...
WIN by Being Changeformational!

**Dr. Jeffrey Magee,
CMC/CBE/CSP/PDM**

Table of Contents

Introduction   7

Section 1: What the Heck is Changeformational?

Chapter 1: Understanding Change   19
Chapter 2: Where Our Change Mindset Develops   27
Chapter 3: The FIST Factor™   37
Chapter 4: The Dangers of Change   49

Section 2: Disruptor

Chapter 5: From Resisting Change to Facilitating   61
            Transformation
Chapter 6: Where is Your Focus?
               Magee Dot Theorem   73
Chapter 7: The Disruption/Interruption Business Cycle™   89
Chapter 8: S.T.O.P. – How to Make Decisions   97
Chapter 9: Accountability   109
Chapter 10: Core Expectations   121

Section 3: Changeformation in Action

Chapter 11: Radical Relevance™   129

Conclusion   139
About the Author   143

"Life is either happening FOR you or it is happening TO you.

You are either working IN your profession/craft/business/life or ON your profession/craft/business/life. You are either adapting to Change or creating Transformation…

The choice is yours!"

Introduction

What the heck is **Changeformational**?

I'll get to that, but first…

Maybe you've heard the line, "If you're not changing, you are dying." The real line should be, *if you're not transforming, you are no longer relevant!*

As an entrepreneur or business owner, the thought of no longer being relevant should terrify you. Irrelevance leads to plummeting sales, and plummeting sales lead to extinction. From there, it's just a matter of time before you end up in the history books as an example of *what not to do;* or worse, your organization is forgotten altogether.

Think about your own business. Do you feel like your competitors are running circles around you? Are they introducing new products or services before you've even identified a need for them? Are their sales skyrocketing while you are doing everything in your power just to keep your head above water?

Or perhaps, until recently, you've had no competition. Maybe you found that special niche where only you existed. Your sales were phenomenal. Your customers were happy, and your employees couldn't wait to come to work each day.

Then *they* arrived. A new company that does everything you do, only better. They serve the same customers you serve, only they make them happier. They hire the same employees you do, and your once-loyal team is now jumping ship. Now, you're clamoring to recapture your market share and return to the glory days.

If any of this sounds familiar, you aren't alone. Thousands of companies have experienced similar upsets.

Look at the trajectory of global business leaders like Woolworths, Montgomery Ward, Sears, Kmart, JCPenney, Blockbuster Video, AOL, and many others. They changed and evolved for decades as markets demanded; yet, as each became complacent, each fizzled out or died. At this time, Amazon is the giant, delivering everything that each of those extinct businesses once owned – Amazon transformed the customer interaction experience and created new rules for everyone else to play by – new rules equal **Changeformational**.

The automotive industry has experienced quite a bit of upset over the years, as well. General Motors was the first billion-dollar global business to lead the automotive world. Unfortunately, from the 1970s to the 1990s, they adopted a "heads down" mentality and built world-class crap. Meanwhile, the Transformational automotive makers of the world were recalibrating how automotive standards would rule the industry. By the time Detroit woke up, most of the global and American automotive world was owned by other players. Every employee who ignored what customers said they *really* wanted (versus what was being offered), is responsible for this downfall. In the end, while Detroit clamored to hold onto the past, many lost their jobs and brands died along the way.

Today, while Detroit produces a great product, it has never understood the "green case" and has lost sight of consumers' preferences. This has allowed Texas-based automakers to transform the market and leave Detroit to play catch up.

Throughout this book, you will see many examples of plain old Change vs. Changeformation in action. I'll refer to the auto industry quite a bit throughout this book because I believe it's very relatable. Whether you work in a white-collar role, or a blue-collar role, or are simply a consumer who has shopped for and owned a vehicle, these examples will hopefully resonate.

There's no doubt you will, at some point (if you have not already), experience a competitor who revolutionizes the industry and "steals" your lead. The only question is whether you will allow this to happen or become **Changeformational** to protect everything you have worked so hard to build.

So, let's start with a few definitions. We will call these our "control factors."

Control Factor One: Change
noun

1: the act, process, or result of changing: such as
a: alteration
b: transformation
c: substitution

Change, it's a billion-dollar industry with Change experts everywhere you look!

Control Factor Two: Transformation
noun

1: an act, process, or instance of transforming
2: the formula that affects a Transformation

Transformation, it's also a billion-dollar industry with Transformation experts everywhere you look!

However, Change is not sufficient. Transformation is not even sufficient. You must thoroughly understand both concepts and apply them universally throughout your organization. You must become **Changeformational**.

You embrace Change and look for ways to evolve it further forward in Transformational ways. **Changeformational** is more than a mindset; it's a strategy, process, and in-your-face action!

When you can truly leverage Change to embrace the big matters of the day, you can make Transformational decisions and take action regarding the Who, What, When, Where, Why, and How of your life and your business.

Before we go any further, allow me to share a little bit about myself.

From my days in corporate America as an award-winning Journalist to selling at the Fortune 100 level, it was clear that everyone is caught up in Change just for the sake of Change, and Change merely to survive – even occasionally, survive very well. As I transitioned into entrepreneurship, owning businesses and leading large teams, it was Transformational thinking and actions that pushed me to the front of the pack and moments of thriving. As I started working on a global level, I recognized it was the best practices and mindset of Change and Transformation melded together that lead to the wins – Changeformational thinking is what the few true leaders possessed.

For many years, I've worked with clients who began by managing Change, then becoming a Change agent or Change advocate, and finally, a Transformational advisor. Throughout this book, I will share what I have learned over decades of experience. By following these principles, you will have the opportunity to win massively at anything you do and blow others away.

Change may be (1) organic, (2) deliberate or (3) forced.
However, when you live in the Change arena,
you are playing by someone else's rules – period.

Having gone from spectator and employee, to manager and leader, then to business owner and investor, I have learned that when you engage only in Change, you can, at best, only survive, never truly Thrive. You will never set new levels with which others will compare and compete – you must become Transformational, as well.

When you set the rules and create new frontiers that others will wish to participate within, you will become the ultimate Transformer. In other words, if you dictate the new rules, others will be forced to play by them.

In this book, I will walk you through what Change is really all about and when it serves your best interests. I will also make the case for why Changeformation is where you must aim, aspire, own, and live with all of your mental DNA and with all of your human capital assets if you are to secure your place today and in your future.

If you read every Change book and blog, consume every Podcast and streaming program, listen to every speaker and professional development program on Change – You will ensure you can remain in the game and

SURVIVE by others' rules…
but you will never THRIVE.

Business models such as lean management, Lean Six-Sigma, agile project management (a.k.a. Scrum in the project-management world), gear you up to play within Change and adhere to others' rules of the game in a most efficient manner. You become a victim of Change: your success is forever dictated by outside factors. When this happens, certain death is just over the horizon.

Yes, Change is a billion-dollar industry, but one with ingrained thoughts, beliefs, and expectations. Fortunately for you, most people are satisfied with following Change rather than leading it. Fortunately for you, you are not "most people."

Through the lens of Changeformation, you can challenge not only yourself and the human capital around you (colleagues, employees, vendors/suppliers/partners, community, etc.), but also your competitors and industry, to step up and in or step out of the conversation and noise of the marketspace today and tomorrow.

At the end of each chapter, you will find exercises titled Prescription to Ensured Success. I encourage you to take the time to do these exercises. These will help you identify the areas in your life and business you need to work on in order to adopt a **Changeformational** Mindset. You'll still benefit from reading the text; however, doing the exercises will help you get ahead faster.

In my global bestseller book, Your Trajectory Code by trade book publisher Wiley, I put forth three calibration application questions at the end of each chapter and found them to be effective. So much so, that several professional trade associations I worked with at the time recalibrated their entire leadership-development ECHO system around my three questions.

If you're ready to become an agent of Changeformation, let's get started!

Section One
What the Heck is Changeformational?

Changeformational is when you are instinctually always evolving, internally and externally, and setting new levels of execution, performance and excellence. It is when you are able to proactively leverage Change and how customers engage with you and others at such a level, that it simultaneously attracts new demographics and changes how existing service, culture, mind-shifts, business, manufacturing, and/or distribution does what it does. Changeformational is when you are able to leverage Change and accelerate Transformation within your organization at a strategic, operational and tactical level .... That's where the true game Changer lives and radiates outward from, as you write the new rules of engagement and business.

It is said that MindShare equals MarketShare and, in this context, how you calibrate your mind to operate is what your mind will see and do. So, if you modify your Mindset to see Change as opportunities and you leverage this for Transformational advances, then you will see more **Changeformational** opportunities where others only see chaos, stress, and begrudged Change initiatives.

Chapter One
Understanding Change

"If it bleeds, it leads."

As a child, I dreamed of being a journalist. I'd interview my family and write "hard-hitting" pieces about my dad's job, what my mom did for a Fortune 500 company, our family vacations, and my neighborhood playmates. I later began working as a general assignment print journalist in Colorado Springs, Colorado, with hundreds of articles appearing in the city's major newspaper, and attending college on journalism and athletic scholarships. I was excited to hone my skills by interviewing and learning from successful individuals and sharing my newfound knowledge with readers.

Unfortunately, as I continued my journalism career in Kansas City after college, my editors had something else in mind. They wanted to see critical and negative articles that showcased the worst aspects of society. I was turned off by their motto, "If it bleeds, it leads," and knew that I had to make a Change. Until I could create my own medium for positive journalism (which I later did with my publication Professional Performance Magazine.), a new career would be needed. That is how I joined the wonderful world of sales.

What Is Change?

Change is the natural and obvious process or evolution we have all been raised within. People tend to like to live within constants, or known parameters, around which they can calibrate their thinking and their actions. In other words, they live within their comfort zone, only stepping out when they are forced to.

Understand that I'm not suggesting Change is bad or inherently limiting. Change is a natural progression, evolution, and state that will take place whether you are mindfully present or not – Change Happens.

When you merely accept Change for what it is and surrender yourself to whatever fate actualizes, then you must also accept ownership of the quality and quantity of what you do and what happens to you. I'm not suggesting that living in a Change state is bad or that an individual who wishes merely to be a contributor in this space is bad – People Happen.

Change is influenced by an unlimited number of variables: from culture, politics, religion, values, laws, morals, goals, economics and the people in our lives, to many more. Understanding these variables will provide insight into the "Change" or "Transformational" modes you can leverage and deploy.

When you feel overwhelmed by circumstances or fearful of what others may inflict upon you, then Change becomes what you allow onto you, and complacency is most often the outcome.

Where Does Change Originate?

Within an organization, Change can originate at the senior leadership level with a decision that trickles down. For example, a new or existing CEO can immediately change culture, strategy, or priority activities and deliverables. Or it could begin with your front-line employees, and work its way up, as when a new employee is hired and brings with them innovation. The question becomes, how does a high-level strategic and structural change impact the operation, process, and activity of your organization? And from there, what does this mean at the tactical daily level for your behaviors, actions, and habits or how they are executed?

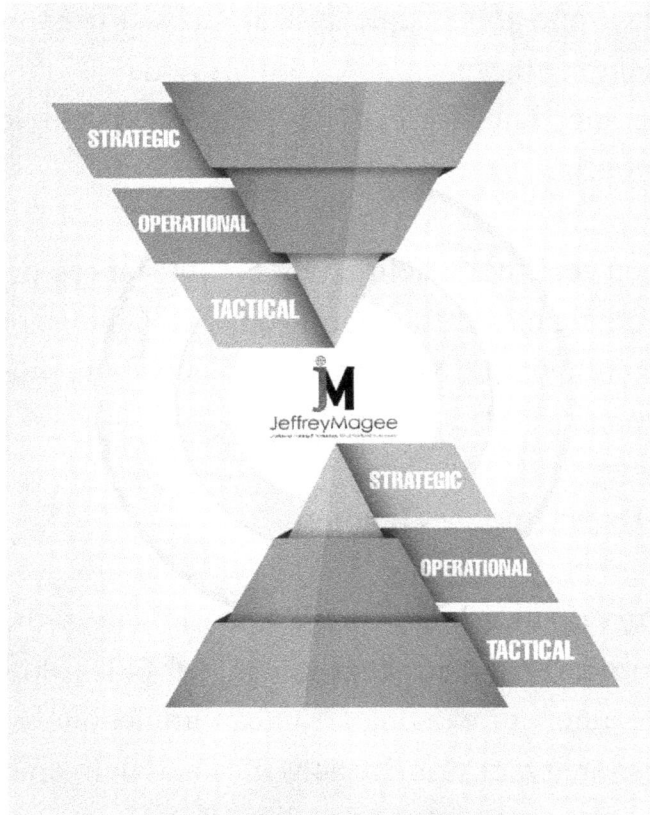

Consider this pyramid that illustrates an organization's labor force. At the top of the pyramid is senior leadership, in the middle is management, and at the base is the employees/staff/team. Consider a change that you are currently facing. From what level did it originate? What will the impact of this change be on you and the other members of your organization?

Now that you recognize where the changes are coming from and how they will impact every level of your organization, you can take a look at how this change may be received by those involved.

The 8 Responses to Change

When we encounter a disruption of our norms, routines, and constants, there is natural pushback. First, seek to gain an understanding of where the pushback is coming from and then explore whether there is an immediate fix or a more long-term solution necessary. When faced with Change, there are 8 typical responses:

1. Avoidance
2. Denial
3. Push Back/Anger
4. Blame/Victimhood
5. Coping
6. Elimination
7. Acceptance
8. Solving & Moving Forward

When faced with Change, the first question someone will ask themselves is, "Does this benefit me?" Depending on the answer to that question, they may have any of the above reactions. Rarely does a positive response garner one of the above responses. In Chapter Seven, we will apply these eight responses to change in business, I call this the **Disruption/Interruption Business Cycle™**.

Why is that? Well, imagine that you work for a company that is not known for doling out more money than it needs to. One day, your boss tells you that you are getting a $75,000 raise. Do you think your boss anticipates pushback? "How dare you! I don't want a raise!"

How about blaming? – "This is all your fault. You are a terrible boss!"

Or coping? – "I don't even know how to deal with this. I need a session with a therapist."

Of course not! The change benefits you; therefore, you are excited about it. Your reaction will be more like a celebration... you might even hug your boss.

On the other hand, if your boss tells you that your salary is being decreased by 20% so he or she can buy a new yacht, you are going to hit many of these responses. You might even hit your boss. (Not recommended.)

Consider how you live in Change in your life now. Are you adapting to and adopting others' rules of the game to exist, or are you engaging others to challenge, question, and address the root cause of Change? Do you find yourself investing a great deal of time with the lower responses? With this knowledge, ask yourself if this behavior accelerates you forward or does it merely weigh you down.

How well you react to Change is based on your Change Mindset. In the next chapter, we will explore where this mindset developed.

Changeformational Prescription to Ensured Success:

1. *As you reflect on what you just read, ask yourself whether you are living and evolving in the context of what you have read and, if so, whether you live in the context of a Change universe.*
2. *As you reflect on what you just read, ask yourself how often you find yourself in any of the eight responses to the Change process and, while there, how much time do you spend or waste in any one response?*
3. *Do you capitalize and leverage Change to place yourself in the lead? If so, you are* ***Changeformational!***

Chapter Two

Where Our Change Mindset Develops

In my teens, two of my high-school classmates and I started a business called Cherry Blossoms, through which we sold advertising to local businesses. (Why did we call it that? I don't have the slightest idea!) Even then I surrounded myself with enterprising individuals who recognized that we could either do what everyone else our age was doing (school, sports, mowing lawns, etc.), or we could craft a different future for ourselves.

One friend had a car, so he was the driver. Another friend was an extrovert, so he was the sales lead. Since it was my idea, I became the business manager.

We went to local businesses around Colorado Springs, Colorado, where we lived, and sold 1/3-page ads from an 8x10 sheet of paper. We could get three ads to a sheet of paper. We then convinced a local printer to print the ads for us at a low price point in exchange for a free ad. We printed them monthly and then invited some of our neighborhood friends to cut up the ads, stuff them into envelopes, and go house to house, placing them in mailboxes.

The advertisers got a great response, so they continued working with us. The printer got new business out of our deal, as well, so he continued to print for us at a low cost, and our friends enjoyed the free pizza and earning a few bucks, so they loved working with us.

Unfortunately, the postman didn't love us quite as much. He informed us that we could not put the envelopes in the mailboxes without stamps.

If we had had a fixed Change Mindset, we would've been unable to see other options and adapt. Adding postage to our ads would've cost too much, and we would've had to close the business. Thankfully, we were ready to transform. We immediately began searching for a new solution. Moving forward, we bypassed the mailboxes and left the ads in people's front doors. Everyone was happy once again, and our business thrived.

Then came the major **Changeformational** breakthrough. Once a year, new telephone books arrived in town. My older brothers knew this and would sign up to be delivery agents: they would get paid to drop new phone books off at home owners' front doors and to business lobby offices.

What a great idea it would be to accompany them and drop off our Cherry Blossom's ad envelopes/packets with them! (In those days phone books did not have ads in them.) People kept the ads with their new phone books and our advertisers got an even greater response. Our new **Changeformational** business was created.

There are two ways that most people look at the world:
1. Life is happening *to you*, or
2. Life is happening *for you*.

The first presumes that you are a victim of your circumstances and, frankly, the world is out to get you. The second option, while slightly better as you see the world conspiring in your favor, is still a very passive position to be in. Do things happen that are outside of our control? Of course! However, for the most part, we don't have to helplessly cling to the tidal waves of life.

What if there was another way to see and interact with the world? What if there was a mindset in which you were *making* life happen? Where you are aware and in control of your future because you are dictating what occurs. This is a **Changeformational** Mindset, and you must strive to be here.

Where Does Our Change Mindset Come From?

If you're not quite there yet, it's understandable. Our Change Mindset was developed in childhood and few people have been empowered with **Changeformational** thinking. We have been conditioned to think the way we think, and act the way we act, based upon the beliefs of those around us. These were (and are) further constricted by the beliefs that manifest as laws of the land and self-designed laws within our head. Laws that are designed to keep us within the "lanes" that others wish us to operate within.

How did your parents approach Change? Whether they outwardly stated their reaction to changes or you simply observed it, you may have seen:

1. A sense of hunker down and protect yourself ... Spending freeze.
2. A sense of anxiety, stress and tension inside the house.
3. A sense of the new unknown taking on a life of its own ... Let's try something new.
4. A sense of defensiveness toward outside subject-matter experts that, on occasion, may enter your family's space ... They could never understand our situation!
5. And, many times, the early stages of Change just simply create a sense of ambiguity that is unsettling ... Just don't know what we should do now.

Whatever your parents' response to Change, you now likely handle Change in a similar way. This has created the billion-dollar industry of Change, influencing the majority to accept and learn how to play within the boundaries dictated by others. While some degree of "Transformational thinking" may appear, it really is not Transformational at all. It is merely the next evolution of the realities that would appear regardless of the players.

How Change Occurs

Before we get much further along, we need to discuss the different ways in which Change occurs. As you read these explanations, compare them to the different ways Change has occurred in your own life.

1. Deliberate – You initiate and are proactive. You are consciously taking an action to evolve something forward to survive and not die and, ideally, be successful within the scope of the Change parameters as to be perceived by others as thriving…. You are deliberate in your decisions to create Change and are being proactive in whatever you do.

2. Forced – You have no choice. You are compelled to do something to survive; You are being made to adjust, adopt, adapt, and change to stay viable or attempt to leverage your uniqueness to survive with the intention to once again Thrive.… You are forced in your decisions to react to or respond to Change, because you either ignored what you could have done or you resisted what you needed to do for so long, that now you must change, whether you like it or not. By doing this you know it will place you where you must be to survive.

3. Organic/Natural – Your standard operating procedures and normal daily workflow drive that happens regardless. The natural evolution of your state, or state of being, that moves forward as it would regardless of any other outside stimulant. At best, you will live a comfortable life surviving the many Change variables that come at you.… You are organically making decisions and dealing with Change due to systems, processes and procedures that really dictate how to react or respond in a Change situation, regardless of individual thought or feelings.

Change, therefore, is a reality and takes place consciously and unconsciously around us 24/7, whether you accept or reject it. Remember ... Change Happens.

And as you live in Change, Transformation or **Changeformational** environments, remember, not everyone will process and embrace Change at the same rate. Most (if not all), people prefer consistency and will experience a range of emotions (as we discussed earlier), when presented with Change. Some will move through those emotions rather quickly. These individuals are **Changeformational**. Others will get bogged down in the "But that's the way it always was..." of the situation and fight to maintain the old.

While the transactional aspects of your life and work are evolutionary and, thus, Change-oriented, for many this is the totality of their life. This can be an overwhelming amount of time consumed. Be mindful that this is merely what I refer to as working IN life and business. To be Transformational and **Changeformational**, you must be mindful to ensure that you are also investing strategic and tactical time working ON your life and business. Working IN means taking care of the expected daily Structure/Systems, Ops, Procedures (SOPs) and routines. When you get to work ON your life and business, you think more macro –

bigger picture – evaluating opportunities otherwise missed, and truly making meaningful impact.

As you read this book, real-life examples will rush through your head. Your homework assignment is to chronicle those examples and the ones presented herein. Go back in your head for first-person references and do the research to understand the backstory to each so you can become **Changeformational**, as well.

Let's take a look at an example that began in Logan, Utah, in 2017.

It's doubtful that consumers were asking for improvements in the cookie industry. As long as cookies (whether through retail stores or mail order), were delicious, not much else mattered. But that wasn't good enough for the founders of Crumbl Cookies. Instead of just starting "another" cookie company, Jason McGowan (CEO) and Sawyer Hemsley (COO) wanted to revolutionize the industry. They took their "perfect cookie quest" to the customers, and once they'd nailed down chocolate chip, they introduced the concept of a rotating menu, trying out new flavors weekly. Customers can watch their cookies being made or they can take advantage of curbside pickup or nationwide shipping. And it's not just a cookie; Crumbl Cookies sells large cookies perfect for sharing. Why? Because they wanted to foster a sense of community. They've now surpassed the 800-store mark, all because they chose to give their customers what they didn't yet know they wanted.

For their **Changeformational** approach, Jason McGowan was recognized at year five of his journey as one of the top CEOs in America by earning the title *EY Entrepreneur of The Year*.

In the next chapter, we will discuss The **FIST Factor** and dive deeper into where our mindset originates and how to change it.

Changeformational Prescription to Ensured Success

1. *As you reflect on what you just read, ask yourself whether you are living and evolving in the context of what you have read and, if so, whether you live in the context of a Change universe.*
2. *As you reflect on what you just read, ask yourself if you are creating the new rules of business based upon the application of what you have just read and are creating game-Changer realities for others to participate with. If so, you are Transformational!*
3. *Do you capitalize and leverage Change to place yourself in the lead? If so, you are* **Changeformational!**
4. *Do you live in the Deliberate? You are living Transformational!*
5. *Do you live in the Organic and/or Forced? You are living in Change!*
6. *Ask yourself, which space is best for you now, and later, and how do you consciously control each?*
7. *If you objectively look around, do you take advantage of the percentage opportunity you need to be successful and THRIVE, by stepping regularly out of being IN focus and spend time ON focused endeavors, people, conversations, initiatives?*

Chapter Three

The FIST Factor™

Do you remember the adage – "Garbage in, Garbage out"?

One of my mentors, advisors and a consistent contributor to www.ProfessionalPerformanceMagazine.com for the past 30 years, Dr. Nido Qubein, President of High Point University and Chairman-of-the-Board for Great Harvest Bread Company, suggested I look at it differently:

Garbage in, garbage stays!
If you consume false, inaccurate or biased views and information, it remains in your mindset and influences your mindware....

Each year, individuals spend countless hours and billions of dollars seeking greater success. So why do some attain high levels of accomplishment while others never seem to get ahead?

If you guessed that successful people are **Changeformational**... you'd be right!

Every person has the same DNA for success or failure in today's global opportunity. The difference between whether you succeed or fail depends on whether you assume ownership of a concept I call the **FIST Factor -**

"5-Critical Influencers on WHO You ARE and Always Will Be," or excuse it away.

For more than three decades, I have worked on the frontline of performance execution and achievement – from global superstars to the person I see in the mirror daily. From serial entrepreneurs and military Generals to solo-business operators, Fortune 100 leaders to Olympic athletes and musicians, from celebrities to bestselling authors and world leaders – all ask me the same two questions:

- "How do I create Change?"

- "Why are some people successful when others are not?"

My answer is always the same. Your ability to be successful boils down to two things:

1. How you have been influenced from birth until today.

2. How you can move beyond those early influences and move forward consciously.

Let's take a look at the factors that determine whether an individual is content to accept Change or whether they are driven to create Transformation.

It does not matter where you come from, what your roots reveal, or where you are going. The **"5-Critical Influencers on WHO You ARE and Always Will Be"** never change. What does change is how you assume ownership of each, manage them and elevate them regularly. These are the influencers who shape you, mentally and physically, during every experience you have or ever will have: the source(s) of all education and influence, fact or rhetoric, logic or revisionist history, and emotional stimulation orbiting within you now, in your past and in your future.

From birth until our last moments on this earth, we are the sum total of every person in our life and their impact upon us. The question is, *who* is in your life?

I'm going to walk you through an exercise I've used with my clients for decades across the world. Flex your hand open, palm up. You have five fingers. Now stop and reflect. At this period in your life, who are the people from whom you:

- Seek mental solace;
- Seek mental guidance and advice; and/or
- Influence how you think, feel, believe and operate.

As you visualize a person, assign them to one of your fingers and keep the countdown going. Assign at least one name per finger. Once you have your five names, you have your FIST factor.

Now, take your fist and slam it into the palm of your opposite hand. Do you feel that power and energy? This is where an individuals' power, strength, energy, self-confidence, and beliefs (or lack thereof), come from. This is how you take ownership to make immediate and sustained Changes in how you think, feel, and behave. This is where you can influence those around you to greatness. Inventory who you have in your head now that shapes your psychology and pathology, and then take ownership of their role in your life.

There are **"5-Critical Influencers on WHO You ARE, and Always Will Be,"** and each one has fostered a different side of your personality and character, so let's identify each and understand who they are:

1. **FAMILY** – You don't get to select your family, but your family is the earliest and potentially most long-lasting influencer. Consider your hand inventory from above; were there any family names that you assigned to a finger or fingers? Do they elevate your game or derail your abilities? Do you embrace them or allow them to hold you back? Are you holding onto toxicity; do YOU need to let go (if not physically, then at least mentally)?

2. **FRIENDS -** You get to select your friends, and they, too, can serve as early and potentially long-lasting influencer groups. Consider your hand inventory from above; were there any friend names you assigned to a finger or fingers? Do they elevate your game or derail your abilities? Do you embrace them or allow them to hold you back? Are you holding onto toxicity; do YOU need to let go?

I've been coaching a local real estate broker for years. He runs an extremely successful agency with 17 teams and more than 120 agents. After having children, he and his wife decided that while they loved their house and appreciated the neighborhood they lived in, the families around them were average. They wanted their children to be surrounded with impressive friends as they grew up. Friends that would lift them up above mediocrity and help them achieve great things. They began their new home search immediately and have never looked back.

3. **PROFESSIONAL CONTACTS** – You get to select your professional key stakeholders, allowing them into your head as early and potentially long-lasting influencers. Consider your hand inventory from above; were there any professional names that you assigned to a finger or fingers? Do they elevate your game or derail your abilities? Do you embrace them or allow them to hold you back? Are you holding onto toxicity; do YOU need to let go?

4. **SUCCESS KEY STAKEHOLDERS** - You get to select the success key stakeholders you allow into your head. Who is the most successful person you actually know? The success category includes that individual you personally know who provides you with meaningful insights and Key Performance

Indicators (KPIs) to replicate and attain accelerated achievement and success in your own trajectories. Consider your hand inventory from above; were there any success names that you assigned to a finger or fingers? Do they elevate your game or derail your abilities? Do you embrace them or allow them to hold you back? Are you holding onto toxicity? Do YOU need to let go?

I have met, interviewed or had many phenomenally successful people participate in my publication, www.ProfessionalPerformanceMagazine.com, over the decades, but if I don't actually know them, they would be a false mental name reference for this category. If I were in need of a mental reference, I would not be able to pull up any first-person interaction and ask myself, what would they do in this situation. I just would not know.

5. **UNDERDOG** – You get to select the underdog key stakeholders you allow into your head. The underdog is someone you know who finds a way to prevail over adversity instead of complaining and blaming. You can learn from their mindsets and behaviors how specific KPIs for success look. You can admire their greatness and be motivated and inspired through them. Consider your hand inventory from above; were there any underdog names that you assigned to a finger or fingers? Do they elevate your game or derail your abilities? Do

you embrace them or allow them to hold you back? Are you holding onto toxicity; do YOU need to let go? Many serial success individuals will say this fifth FIST factor influencer is the most powerful for the body armor you need to sustain life success!

Each core category illustrates how the differing critical influencers affect you: how your thinking has been influenced and may still be influenced, and how you may experience and see the environment around you. The diversity of thought shapes the diversity of how you may see and address Change and Transformation within and around yourself. And, with this simple categorization that allows you to see the life journey influencers on others, it acts as a reference point for yourself, as well. Now, here is the power of the concept: to unleash your **Changeformational** DNA today and tomorrow, consider these five influence points and the influences radiating from each, if any hold you back or inhibit your ability to survive in Change or Thrive in Transformation, it is time to replace those influencers with new ones.

When it comes to allowing people into your life, consider your future associations strategically through a mental- and physical-health perspective. They will be key influencers on who you are and will become, so choose wisely.

How many people did you initially inventory in your **FIST Factor**? Are there multiple names in any one influence category? Only you can determine if that number is acceptable, too many, or not enough. Do you have any influence categories without names? If so, you are out of balance with the **"5-Critical Influencers on WHO You ARE and Always Will Be."** While there may not be an exact or correct number of names you want in any one influence category, you do want to ensure you have power names in each influence category for balance of perspective and better accountability partners.

Now, let's dramatically elevate this **FIST Factor** concept. Think of these five categories as encompassing your key influencers, and let's shift the name *from* **FIST Factor** *to* Board of Directors or Advisory Board. You need representation in each influence category to have a balanced and accountable internal dialogue or outward discussion on any factor in life and to elevate your game and ensure you're not being influenced disproportionately in an ill-advised direction.

Every aspect of your life has been shaped, influenced, and/or guided by one or more of these five influencer groups. How you engage with them in your future will reinforce your beliefs and actions or challenge them, accordingly.

If you don't like what your present FIST Factor reveals,
Change up the influencers within your FIST Factor
today!

To achieve balance within your **FIST Factor** (a.k.a. Board of Directors or Advisory Board), first, ensure you have representation in each of the five influencer categories.

Your consciousness, including unconscious bias or not, objectivity and desire for critical analysis capabilities, not just your self-validation, will be directly influenced by the diversity and balance of viable, "legitimate" influencers!

Elevate your life trajectory, as I call it in my bestselling book, Your Trajectory Code, (www.JeffreyMagee.com). For any next-level goal you have, reflect upon your **FIST Factor**, and ask whether they will get you where you want to go? If so, leverage them and their imprints on your psychology. If you need to expand your five critical influence categories with new people, expand your network.

An engaged **FIST Factor** of individuals, with multiple occupants in each influence category, empowers you to stand soundly when making decisions and forging future-focused actions.

To recognize the unconscious or conscious influence from the individuals you inventoried, ask yourself the following reference question:

1. For the past year, consider: where do I live, where do I shop for groceries and where do I work? Any change in the makeup of my inventory of influencers?

2. For the past five years, consider: where have I lived, where did I shop for groceries and where did I work? Any change in the makeup of my inventory of influencers?

3. For the past decade, consider: where did I live, where did I shop for groceries and where did I work? Any change in the makeup of my inventory of influencers?

Want to create meaningful Change? Consider who you allow to provide input, influence, and healthy challenge in your life. Everyone has an agenda, so determine whether an influencer's agenda is serving you or working against you.

If you have a toxic member on your Board of Directors, you should fire them. It's time to unleash yourself from those who no longer provide value to you and replace them with conscious contributors to your life!

Entrepreneur, author, and motivational speaker Jim Rohn once famously stated, "You are the average of the five people you spend the most time with."

Elevating your mental DNA and how you see, manage, and leverage opportunities to be Changeformational begins with how you have been influenced in the past. You can actively adjust your FIST Factor to be even better in the future. Consider these five people that the late Jim Rohn referenced come from among the five demographics of your FIST FACTOR. So now this becomes compounded by the five within the five for as many as 25-plus calibrators of who you are and whom you can become. If you are leading others, it is you plus them, plus their five, that affords you the ability to survive, thrive and or win!

So, where are you? Where is your organization? We all have **"5-Critical Influencers on WHO You ARE and Always Will Be**." The only difference is whether you take control of or surrender your **FIST Factor** and who you can become!

Changeformational Prescription to Ensured Success

1. *As you reflect on what you just read, ask yourself whether you are living and evolving in the context of what you have read and, if so, whether you live in the context of a Change universe.*

2. *As you reflect on what you just read, ask yourself whether you are creating the new rules of business based upon the application of what you have just read and whether you are creating game-Changer realities for others to participate within. If so, you are Transformational!*

3. *Do you capitalize and leverage Change to place yourself in the lead? If so, you are **Changeformational!***

4. *For you to ensure your **Changeformational** Mindset is focused, do you have constructive advocates on your mental Board of Directors, your **FIST Factor**, who have the capacity to elevate and accelerate your success?*

5. *Do these people challenge you forward regularly and can you confirm that they have that accelerant factor, what some would call a Force Multiplier?*

6. *Are you willing to radically mix up this network and invite new talent into the mix? Maybe people that you would have previously not considered? If so, you are becoming Transformational. If you're not that much of a risk taker yet and want to just evolve the **FIST Factor** you have, then Change is where you live.*

Chapter Four
The Dangers of Change

We have lived with Change disciples and Change programs, so why do so few survive Change and go on to Thrive?

Simple... Change is always a game of catch-up.

And sometimes, Change is also created by disingenuous people for their personal agenda, regardless of the trauma it may inflict on others.

The Great Global Reboot (aka Covid) shined a spotlight on the businesses that thrived during this time (and beyond). It helped us realize such organizations were actually engaged in **Changeformational** strategies, thinking, and execution. Similar businesses that merely engaged in Change, found themselves surviving and/or dying in this same time period. Today, major think tanks, leading organizational Change agents, and consulting firms are busy publishing what you must be doing to survive or Thrive... yet they are simply parroting others' best practices. These are the same old Change ideas and they are no longer sufficient.

I'm reminded of a classic **Changeformationalist™** Mindset example provided by the leading global Business Consultant, Dr. Alan Weiss. Throughout Covid, American automakers were unable to build new cars due to the global microchip shortage and had to slow down, or outright shut down, production as a result. Elon Musk doubled down as a Transformationalist and showed his team and the industry how to win.

How?

When his engineers indicated they, too, needed new microchips for their car manufacturing production lines and could not secure them, Musk directed them to instead rewrite the codes for the new cars to be compatible with the old or existing microchips (of which they had a surplus). No longer were they held hostage by supply-chain issues. Instead, Tesla won, with more cars produced and sold during Covid than ever before – and in California for this time period, they were the #2 automotive manufacturer!

When we evaluate business wins, losses, and draws of the past 100 years, those that won had Transformation DNA KPIs. While those on the losing and draw side competed within the Change DNA KPI arena.

The global and American business frontier is littered with historical examples of **Changeformationalist** icons. Consider Ben Franklin Five-and-Dime stores, Woolworth's, Montgomery Ward, Sears, Kmart, and JCPenney; each was **Changeformational** for a period of time, disrupting an existing market-and-supply chain. Yet, each became complacent. Exhausted by Change measures to stay relevant, they finally became extinct.

These businesses *should* be in Amazon's position right now. They had the inventory, the suppliers, product data in a computer system, massive customer contact lists/data/analytics, and the brand. But they forgot the DNA of Transformation that built them and chose to play in the market of Change, living a slow death until their natural end state.

Let's take a closer look at Sears. It was **Changeformational** in its infancy. Sears had the consumer market share, they had the main street USA retail store outlets, a catalog following, consumer contact data and metrics, and distribution centers and they owned the supply-chain system. Yet, they never saw the market evolution and customer interaction needs coming ... They never saw the outward facing consumer from their perspective until it was too late.

This plays across every industry and geography throughout time.

Sometimes, those who are **Changeformational**, become comfortable and merely Transformational. Then, the comfort and complacency drive them to become merely capable Change players, and it's a downward spiral to survivalist mode and playing catch up. Far too often, it's too late and it's off to the ash heaps of once-great business giants and business history footnotes.

Look at yourself and ask whether you actually operate at peak performance when things are static, when you are evolving, or when you seek the bursts of greatness opportunities?

When you can morph from Change Mindset to Transformational Mindset, and be able to maintain the best of both – you are a **Changeformationalist**.

Here are just some of the traits of each:

Change	Changeformational
Follower/Manager	*Leader/Executive*
Hesitation	Anticipation
Evokes Fear	Drives Innovation
Evokes Anxiety	Creates Creativity
Evokes Resistance	Empowers Resiliency
Creates Standoffishness	Embraces Potentiality
Can Be Negative	Drives Positiveness
Following Others	Leading Others
Maintenance Mindset	Engine of Evolution Mindset
Reactive	Proactive
Resistance	Ownership
Best-Practice Mindset	Better-Practice Mindset
Benchmark of Others	Sets Benchmark for Others
Finite Mindset	Infinite/Abundance Mindset
Change Management	Transformational Strategist
Transactional	Relational
Process Driven	Strategic Focus
Present/Past-Tense Focus	Future-Tense-Focused Opportunities
Subjective Focus	Outcome Focus
Rearview Mirror Energy	Windshield View Energy

Catching-Up KPIs	Setting-the-Pathway KPIs
Responsive	Disruptive
Applier	Innovator
Looking for a Piece of the Pie	Reinventing and Enlarging the Pie
Merging with Others	Collaborating and Leading Others
Selling Out	Buying Others
Managing Your Teams	Leveraging Human Capital
How to be LEAN Mindset	Pushing LEAN to New Levels
Resource Management	Resource Reapplication
Settling into the Rules	Visionary
Hostage to Supply Chain	Owns Supply Chain
Responds to Disruptions	Creates & Anticipates Disruptions
Anxiety	Anticipation
Live by Rules	Write/Rewrite the Rules
Live by Change Agents	Engage Trusted Advisors
Preparing for what you expect next	Creating what everyone isn't ready for
Understanding Trends and Evolution	Creating the Trends & Next Evolution
Capitalizing upon Change	Seeing what everyone else misses
Adapts, Adopts, and Adjusts	Leverages Abundance Mentality
Creates Outliers	Attracts Alignment of Others
Defends Existing Habits	Welcomes Evolving New Habits

Now, consider the DNA characteristics of Change and the DNA characteristics of Transformational within your own business and within yourself? Where are you and your organization? Do your responses fall into the Change or **Changeformational** category?

So ask yourself, who are you? Are you in the pack or do you create the pack? Are you *in the* market or establishing the rules *of the* market? Are you the disruptor and innovator or dreading the interruption, disruption, and innovation from other brands that your team is positioned to respond to?

Ready to laugh? In the Introduction, you read about how the auto industry has failed, time and time again, to be **Changeformational**. Let's look at some undeniable proof that every company is just following in the footsteps of the others....

Dodge  Chevrolet

Lincoln  Honda

Buick  Mercedes

Ford  Infiniti

Nissan  Hyundai

Porsche  BMW

BMW  Toyota

It's time to elevate the mental DNA of those around you: those you lead, those you hire and those you want to play the game of life with you. Ask each to evaluate everything you/they do. Assess and ask others (as well as yourself regularly), about that which you design, manufacture, distribute, facilitate, do, etc. and see how it can be *Changeformationally* elevated to new levels.

A simple Rule of Four to get your **Changeformational** juices flowing. Anything you do, offer, or participate in, ask:

1. How can it be BETTER?
2. How can it be FASTER or more EFFICIENT?
3. How can it be DIFFERENT to serve the next evolution of the market?
4. How can it be more COST EFFECTIVE? (And that does not mean cheaper.)

Stop trying to Change and begin to Transform. Elevate and accelerate beyond others as a **Changeformationalist!**

Larger organizations and government entities have the capacity to employ and deploy Transformational thinkers, innovators and creators of future realities. In many cases this is the old school Research & Development (R&D) enterprises. It was this team's mandate to challenge the status quo and explore the deliverable of the future and the customer of the future, both of which are not in your current present state.

To truly survive and Thrive in the marketplace of today and tomorrow, everyone, all the way down to the granular individual level, must be capable of thinking and operating as a **Changeformationalist!**

Change is dangerous. Stop being satisfied with mediocrity. Changeformation will take you to great destinations, innovation and success.

> ***Changeformational Prescription to Ensured Success***
>
> 1. *As you reflect on what you just read, ask yourself whether you are living and evolving in the context of a Change universe.*
> 2. *As you reflect on what you just read, ask yourself whether you are creating the new rules of business and creating game-changer realities for others to participate within. If so, you are Transformational!*
> 3. *Do you capitalize and leverage Change to place yourself in the lead. If so, you are* **Changeformational!**
> 4. *Assess yourself from the lens of the* **Changeformational** *checklist: do you tend to have more Change or more Transformational traits or characteristics?*
> 5. *To push yourself beyond Change and to begin to think and write the new rules of engagement, apply the Rule of Four against anything you do and anything you produce, market, distribute, etc. in the marketplace today.*

Section Two
Being a Disruptor

You're a Disruptor when you stimulate others to Change because they must evolve their KPIs to be DIFFERENT, BETTER, FASTER, and more COST EFFECTIVE to survive ...

Challenging yourself out of acceptance and complacency into action and Transformation starts with the mindset you possess and the mindset of those around you. Change matters and the urgency to transform to Transformational thinking and acting is even more critical. Consider the ABCs of managing Change for performance impact!

Chapter Five
From Resisting Change to Facilitating Transformation

You've likely heard the adage, "Change is the only constant in life." Well, the same is true for business.

Psychology reveals that individuals and groups will change a behavior, action, or opinion for one of only two core reasons: avoiding pain or seeking pleasure, which we will discuss shortly. Without one of these two reasons, human nature is to resist Change and remain complacent. As a result, leaders wait to evolve until it's almost too late, often finding themselves struggling to impose Change on their team or employees. This leads to resentment, poor performance, and loss of revenue.

A model that I have found very effective in accelerating Transformational thinking and actions, as opposed to dealing with constant Change, is the Trajectory Code Model.

To fast-track Change in a world that may (for some), be moving too fast, consider these three steps for performance execution (implementation) success and blend them into the new **ABC (A+B=C) Model** for Transformation and what I refer to as the Trajectory Code. Consider:

1. **A = The ACTIVATING event or Stimulant** (and there will always be one), is the starting point.

2. **B = Your BEHAVIOR** and actions are associated with or blended into the Activating Events, which can guide you into a state of complacent behaviors if unchecked. This breeds habits that mold your personal operational styles, which then feed your (incorrect) emotional belief that you are at peak performance and doing everything right.

3. **C = CALIBRATED CIRCUMSTANCES,** or the desired outcome, goals, objectives, or success, based off of measurable KPIs.

Whether your reality is the merging of organizations to survive and Thrive in the future or blending your once solo abilities with another for combined synergy and success, these three paths will help you get there. So let's take this elementary psychology model used in business and life, and now apply it to the Trajectory Code Model.

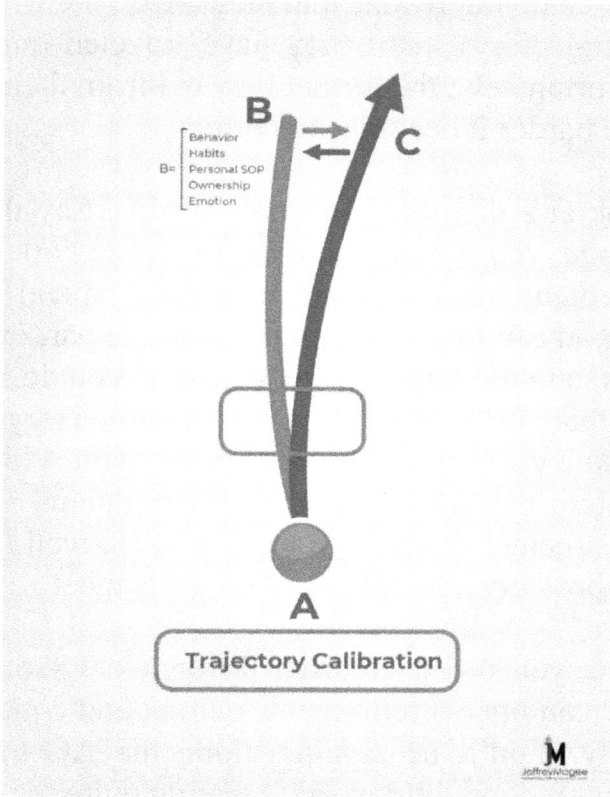

B =
- Behavior
- Habits
- Personal SOP
- Ownership
- Emotion

Trajectory Calibration

This formula has been Transformational for my business and for many of my clients. I trust that it will help you, too.

Your starting point is always A.
B is the point of failure. The road from A to B is paved with poor decisions and missteps.
C is the point of success. The road from A to C is infinite.

People often do not realize that they are on the wrong path (an AB trajectory), until they have traveled quite some way. Unfortunately, the further they get from their starting point, the harder it becomes to correct.

Let's look at a digestible example of this. Say that at 25 years of age, you decide you want to retire at 60. You can do what many twenty-somethings do... spend all your money. You can invest in nights out at the bar, expensive vacations, and the latest gadget or car. If you do, you will discover that you're traveling on an AB trajectory. Having put no money towards your retirement, you will have to play catchup in your 40s, dumping large sums of money into investments, or you will have to work well into your 70s (and possibly beyond), to make ends meet.

Of course, you could do what fewer twenty-somethings do... you can open a retirement account and contribute to it monthly. You'll be zipping along the AC trajectory, earning compound interest and creating quite the nest egg for your future.

As you use this model and incorporate it into your lexicon, you want to identify every KPI as a marker in order to discern if your actions are on an ultimate AB Trajectory or an ultimate AC Trajectory.

I like to share with my clients and audiences that the difference between failure or derailment and success is actually nothing. This gets people's attention so I can explain. There are five levels of "behavior." (I know some of what I am about to list are not actually behaviors.)

Notice that as we all leave a Point A in life, we are introduced to how to do something. That is behavior and behavior is a conscious mental state. The more we do this behavior, it manifests into a habit, which is a subconscious state of mind. After a period of doing this habit, it manifests into what I call a personalized SOP. This is where you take ownership of your own way of seeing, believing, and doing. At this fourth level, we then wrap our emotional state around our SOP and, typically, push away everyone and everything that is not consistent with our mental state of being.

Here is where Change then becomes a challenge for individuals and organizations. If we can take these same five behavior states and move them from the AB Trajectory to the AC Trajectory, we can deal with Change more effectively and even leverage it into states of Transformation and, thus, become **Changeformationalists**.

And, back to the earlier statement: the difference between failure/derailment and success is nothing. You will act out these five levels of behavior. The question is merely, will you allow this to work unconsciously against you in an AB Trajectory or realize these five levels of behavior will occur regardless, and so make them conscious and AC Trajectory actions?

Change is important to any person or organization as it evolves. Get your team on board with the ABCs of managing Change and learn how you can better engage individuals to help them embrace growth!

Transformation, however, is where you must be to elevate those around you in life or in business to new heights of success that they may not have ever on their own been able to visualize and realize!

Now recognize in the diagram, directly above the letter A dot is a circular oval with line AB and line AC going through it. Imagine that letter A as a thumbtack on a wall with two threads hanging from it. If you grabbed one thread and tacked it on letter B and then tacked the second thread on letter C, the two threads, as they leave letter A, would be somewhat on top of each other. It would only be as the threads went further upward that you could actually see them separating. I call that overlap the One-Percent Factor. If you can recognize what is happening or what you are doing closer to point A and extrapolate outward to determine whether your behavior will take you to Point B or C, you can make a mere one-percent recalibration to ensure you are working toward Point C.

One of the ways you can evaluate how you think about Transformation, how you see those around you, and how you are influenced to accelerate towards greater AC Trajectory outcomes, is to understand Rule 80-10-10™ and the myriad applications this has upon us.

Let's apply **Rule 80-10-10** (Gallup's 56-15-29 analysis of demographics as discussed below), to identify Change agents. When you look at any organization, group of people, or demographic, that large whole always breaks down into three initial subsets. When you understand how the two smaller demographics influence the much larger demographic, you understand the reality of Changeformation.

1. **Followers – 80 Percent** of any group, at the outset, typically falls into a sub-demographic of Followers. They will lean in the direction they are influenced into.... It is easy to create momentum in Change when you can enlist and recruit 80 percent of a group to fall in behind you.

So, who does the influencing? (Transformationalists)

2. **Transformers – 10 Percent** of any group, at the outset, typically falls into a sub-demographic of Transformers. These people have the capacity to influence and transform the mindsets of Followers to recruit them to your cause. There are two immediate ways to identify and recruit a Transformer to your cause:
   a. A Transformer has a vested interest in your cause.
   b. You already have a positive connection with someone. Therefore, they'd make a great Transformer.

3. **Terrorists – 10 Percent** of any group, at the outset, typically falls into a sub-demographic of Terrorists. They have the capacity to influence and change the mindset of Followers to recruit them to their cause. There are two immediate ways to identify a Terrorist:

   a. A Terrorist has no vested interest in your cause.

   b. You have a negative connection with someone or they do not like your forward-focused plans (because they live to go backward). These people are Terrorists and blame anyone that threatens their status quo.

You can see this model play out by watching the advertising and marketing dollars of businesses in play. Or by watching political leaders; how they present messaging or present influencers in their messaging to lead people to follow them.

Recently, the Gallup organization did global research and found statistically the same three subgroups present within any organization and throughout society. Their more precise numbers:

1. **56 Percent** of any demographic on any given day is identified as "Disengaged/Complacent" … I call

this group the Followers. Not to be classified as good nor bad, merely individuals who need to be engaged, valued, appreciated and meaningfully lead to Transformational greatness. Left alone to their own devices, they are susceptible to influence by one of two influencer subgroups or demographics: Transformers and Terrorists.

So, who does the influencing? (Transformationalists)

2. **29 Percent** of any demographic on any given day is identified as "Actively Engaged" … I call these the Transformers. These people have the capacity to influence and transform the mindsets of the Followers. There are two immediate ways to identify and recruit a Transformer to your cause:
    a. Find someone with a vested interest in your cause.
    b. Look for someone with whom you already have a connection or relationship.

3. **15 Percent** of any demographic on any given day is identified as "Actively Disengaged" … I call these Terrorists. These people see your ideas as a threat to their power and influence, or they just don't like you. Terrorists have the capacity to influence and

change the mindset of the 56-Percenters. There are two immediate ways to identify a Terrorist:

a. Find those who have no vested interest in your cause.
b. Identify the individuals that just do not like you or your forward-focused plans. They live to go backward and blame anyone that threatens their status quo.

A Culture of Changeformation from top-down and down-up is now a reality that you can create.

Changeformational Prescription to Ensured Success

1. *As you reflect on what you just read, ask yourself whether you are living and evolving in the context of what you have read and, if so, whether you live in the context of a Change universe.*

2. *As you reflect on what you just read, ask yourself whether you are creating the new rules of business based upon the application of what you have just read and are creating game-changer realities for others to participate within. If so, you are Transformational!*

3. *Do you capitalize and leverage Change to place yourself in the lead? If so, you are* **Changeformational!**

4. *When you deal with Change, are you accepting and engaging or challenging and resistant?*

5. *How do you calibrate your mind, or other minds, to accept Change more quickly (consider ways you can use the 3-step model presented in the beginning of this Chapter)?*

6. *Can you use the ABCs of the Trajectory Code Model right now – be Transformational?*

7. *To be* **Changeformational***, surround yourself with the 29-percent factor (a.k.a. the 10 percent), the Transformers.*

8. *Hire, onboard, engage, support and develop a culture and environment that repels the 15 percent who are Actively Disengaged (a.k.a. the 10 percent), Terrorists.*

Chapter Six
Where is Your Focus?
Magee Dot Theorem

Situational Awareness = Strategic Effectiveness!
Living in Change denies you of this understanding and living in Transformation encourages this superpower within yourself.

I had just finished giving a series of leadership trainings to one of my corporate clients when the CEO stepped up to the front of the room. He stopped in front of the flipchart, turned to a blank page, and with a dark-colored marker, drew a large dot in the center of the paper.

"What do you see?" He asked the audience.

●

And now, I'll ask you, "What do you see?"

The majority of responders say they see a dot, while only a small percentage will say white space.

Don't worry, there is no incorrect answer. However, your answer reveals if you are inwardly or outwardly focused.

"The mental tools Dr. Jeff has just presented can only serve us as leaders if we first understand our orientation," explained the CEO. "What most people see and fixate on in life are the dots, and that can be situationally good. Great taskers and managers live here. But if you see the white space, you can create, innovate, and transform."

And it hit me! When you can see the dot *and* the white space, that is where great leaders live! Changeformational!

I sat there, nursing my coffee and allowing this idea to percolate in my head. Since that day, I have held strong to this as a theory to greater success. Challenge yourself and reflect on where you live. What did you see first, the dot or the white space? What are your natural tendencies and conditioning? What are those of your peers at work?

DOTS *Follower/Manager*	WHITE SPACE *Leader/Executive*
Tasks	Opportunities
Goal	Horizon
Objective	Innovation
Purpose	Creativity
Agenda	Pushing the limits
Deliverable	What Others Don't See
Product	Collaborations
Tangible	Unforeseen Collaborations
KPIs	A Whole New Scorecard
Rules	New Alignments
Policies	Exceptions
Guidelines	Next Generation
SOPs	Reinvention

I have come to call this the **Magee DOT Theorem** and have grown it exponentially. Allow me to share. Most everyone gets so fixated on the dot, they don't see Change coming and are always looking for ways to use their dots and/or gently evolve their dots so they can stay in the game. Dots are sometimes used to deflect and distract you away from what is coming and what you should be focused upon. When you move to the white space, you see what everyone else is missing. When you can see beyond the borders of the white space, from your intuition, instincts, wisdom, experience, and knowledge and predict what's next and/or create what's next, you become **Changeformational**.

While being a dot-centric thinker or a white-space innovative thinker may be your dominant psychology, you can step outside yourself when you recognize where you are and what is needed. But don't deny your highly developed self, either. There is power in following your natural instincts.

The more you focus on the dots, the more you will live in Change constants. The more you can explore white space, the sooner you can become Transformational. When you can blend and leverage both dots and space, you are **Changeformational!**

Here is a classic example from the last two decades: Lee Iacocca changed the automotive world to be what every reader of this book has experienced, whether you realized it or not. He was **Changeformational**; he evolved the entire automotive world as we know it today to where it is now (and Elon Musk would be the Lee Iacocca of today). Quick history lesson: when Iacocca assumed the CEO position at Chrysler, they and the other all-American automotive makers were on the brink of bankruptcy. He challenged his designers. The station wagon was for women and the van was for men, yet neither were buying either vehicle. The need for both was there so he told them, "Don't make either bigger, better, faster, or different." (Because that would be Change). He challenged them to come up with something truly Transformational. The minivan was born, and everyone followed suit. But what came from that was altogether **Changeformational**... the SUV.

Today, though, very few auto CEOs are Transformational. Instead, they are stuck in the Change loop trying to survive. Occasionally one car may thrive, with a simple forward-thinking adaptation, only to be passed by another. Change does create variations, but it tends to be merely variations on the same ONE thing.

Need a few examples of **Changeformational** businesses?

1. Yum! Brands® revolutionized the fast-food restaurant industry when it realized that changing the aesthetics of a building did very little to impact the bottom line. However, there was one thing that could provide an excellent Return on Investment, (ROI): they realized they could save time and money by housing multiple restaurants in one building (for example: a Taco Bell, a KFC and a Pizza Hut all in one). They had to think beyond having one restaurant per building, each with their own staff and supply chain – **Changeformational!**

2. When the U.S. Postal Service recognized it needed to be where the customers were and started placing USPS offices into gas stations, selling stamps at ATM cash machines, offering 24/7 delivery to homes, and empowering their delivery service professionals to get to know their customers – **Changeformational!**

3. When the introduction of smartphone apps appeared in the technology world, from the consumer's perspective it was not a Change evolution, it was Transformation since it impacted every industry, introducing a new way of engaging the market and doing business – **Changeformational!**

Changeformational is when the legal industry participates by creating a law, so they can then follow that up with massive billion-dollar lawsuits against an industry or the government.

You've probably seen a great example of this post-Covid, without even knowing it was happening. Have you seen the commercials regarding The Camp Lejeune toxic water issues? From the 1950s to the 1980s, people who lived and worked at Camp Lejeune, a U.S. Marine Corps Base in North Carolina, were exposed to contaminated drinking water. A dry-cleaning business off-base was using improper waste disposal practices and leeching dangerous chemicals into the water. Chemicals that would eventually cause cancer in many of the people exposed. There are commercials inviting those who were at this location between x and y dates to contact the law firm so they can sue the Federal Government on the victim's behalf.

Normally, military personnel can't sue the government. However, a group of law firms melded together to write legislation known as the Promise to Address Comprehensive Toxics Act of 2022, and then shipped it to Congressional leaders to act upon it and turn it into a law.

Tesla is **Changeformational** in making the electric vehicle a vehicle for the masses and challenging conventional wisdom. (Although it still uses conventional energy sources to come through the wire to charge it – oops!)

When I reflect upon my life, I see with great clarity the differing times when I was living in Change, whether it was organic Change, forced Change or deliberate Change. I am sure you can, as well. In the 1980s, I had the opportunity to work as a Territory Sales Representative for a Fortune 100 Firm, Boyle-Midway, a consumer products firm. While there were many great opportunities and experiences afforded to me, one of the greatest was about believing in yourself and always banking on yourself, no one else. Not long after returning from a National Sales Conference in Orlando with thousands of colleagues, having been recognized as one of the top Territory Sales Representatives in the nation, I was terminated. What I subsequently learned was that my Area Sales Manager was insecure and intimidated by others around him. He'd make little comments around me, but I let them slide. Once, in a meeting, he commented that he wanted to be the first Area Manager to have an all-female sales team. Another time he commented that I knew what I was doing, so he did not need to spend as much time with me in the field. He forged my signature for months on ride-along documents to make the case for termination due to "insubordination" and "failure to make changes", as advised. While I had all the documentation to support my position, when I talked with legal counsel, their words pierced my brain: "… while this is very unfortunate, here is the reality. YOU are young, you are white, you are male, and you were gainfully reemployed in less than a week. No jury in the world cares. If any of these first variables were different, we would have a case. Consider this a life lesson and move on."

And I did. I began paying attention to even the little comments and actions of others. Recognize that when something does not seem right or feel right, consider what is happening around you and document everything you can. This can be a proactive catalyst to being deliberate in the Changes around you.

I can identify similar situations where I noticed, over the span of my life, those impending Changes coming at me making massive trajectory calibration Changes, transforming my life. I am sure you can, as well.

Many years ago, in my present business JeffreyMagee.com, I realized that my purpose is to work with other professionals and business leaders to make major strides forward, sustain innovative Change, make Transformations in their businesses exciting and rewarding for everyone, and create great places to be/work through positive leadership. So I created, not a training platform of programs from my intellectual capital that could be picked and deployed as seen fit, but an experience. A journey and a programmed approach, whereby I come in and work with the client for a minimum of one year. This has become **Changeformational**. And what I have recognized over the past few decades is that many organizations, institutions, and people have changed their approach to follow my LEADERSHIP MASTERY: LEADERSHIP ACADEMY OF EXCELLENCE/1.0-3.0

Series and my SALES MASTERY: PERFORMANCE DRIVEN SELLING/1.0-8.0 Series formulas!

Current Habits + Current Technology + Current SOP (Structure/Systems, Ops, Procedures) = Current Predictability & Expectations you have come to rely upon....

Dramatically Altered Outcomes/Advances/Consequences occur when you alter any part of the formula....

Now, let's take the concept of focus a little bit further.

Imagine you are in a time machine. Not the traditional time machine like in <u>Back to the Future,</u> where you could potentially unravel the very fabric of the space/time continuum. No, while this time machine looks like a car, it only allows you to reflect upon the seasons of your life, past, present, and future. (And it may just help you move from a dot focus to a white-space focus.)

Now, where you sit or stand is the present time, but where you place your dominant focus will tell you a lot about whether you are dying, surviving, or thriving.

What is your autopilot tendency? Where do your dominant mental and physical energies and attention go? Another way to look at this is, what percentage of time do you spend doing the following:

1. Looking in the Rearview Mirror of Life. Reliving, ad nauseum, past successes or failures. Recycling on what did not go your way, the missed opportunities, the what ifs, should haves, and all the-bad-crap-in-your-life archives? Here is where you will find minimal success in your future life and Change will dominate your life. You will always be playing in someone else's arena of life.

   What is amazing is that the Rearview Mirror occupies such a small space, yet for many, it is where the dominant energy goes. These are Change creatures. Reach up and grab that Rearview Mirror and rip it off and throw it out your window. Let's start fixating upon Transformational DNA. (Note: don't actually do this to your car's rearview mirror. You'll need that to drive.)

   The more time you spend looking in your Rearview Mirror (or surrounding yourself with those who do), the more difficult it will be to accelerate forward. Living someone else's Change model will be your reality if you live in the comfort of your Rearview Mirror!

83

The Rearview Mirror is where the haters, doubters, skeptics, and jealous people live. They will always be ready to point out why you are wrong or can't do something. They live for their misery and want everyone else in their club. They are happy to provide an endless list of excuses for how they have been wronged and will gladly share them with you!

2. Looking in the Side Mirror of Life on our time machine. This mirror is important because it does not dominate your time and it allows you to see what happened behind you, but only a short glance for reference. It also elevates your attention to what may be coming alongside you to instigate a Change or Transformation. Use the Side Mirror for occasional benchmarking, lessons learned, and Aha! moments, but never let it dominate your attention.

3. Looking at the Windshield of Life and the endless opportunities before you. This is where you can be ahead of the pack and create the Change loops coming at you. What you see that others do not, is where Transformation lies. You can't accelerate forward to be **Changeformational**, if you're being distracted away from the Windshield by Rearview

Mirror and Side Mirror issues, conversations and re-looping memories – hey, your high-school state championship is over, move on!

The Windshield is where you find those who encourage you, champion you, believe in you, advocate for you and give clarity to the impact you have and degree of Transformation you can actually achieve!

4. Looking at the Dashboard of Life. In order to assess whether you (and those around you), are geared for Transformation, reflect on your Dashboard of Life. Can you accelerate forward without even looking out of the Windshield of Life because your Dashboard insights, optics and analytics are so precision-tuned?

Your Dashboard pulls into consideration every concept that you have read in this book thus far and what's in the coming pages. It draws upon your years of experience and intuition. And most importantly, upon your ability to unleash that creative DNA within you and others to see beyond the Windshield, via your Dashboard, opportunities not yet visible to others.

A most important note: your Dashboard must provide objective optics and be void of bias, prejudice, and "BS" to be relevant today and tomorrow.

Step out of the business world for a moment and imagine you are a downhill skier. It's an exhilarating, though mildly dangerous, sport. Do you know what makes it more dangerous? Taking your eyes off the path in front of you to look at what's behind or beside you. Trees don't pop out of nowhere. If you're looking forward, you've got plenty of time to see them and navigate around them. The same is true of business.

As a business person, you should spend 75% of your time looking through the Windshield at what's in front of you, 20% of your time looking at the Side Mirror to understand what's going on around you in life and in the marketplace, and 5% of the time looking out the Rearview Mirror at your history.

Many times, the Transformational player and, thus the **Changeformational** winner, is merely listening, watching and paying attention. Today, very few do these three actions. Prove it to yourself: watch and observe others. Everyone today is an instant consumer of what the loudest voice yells (on social media, news or around you), regardless of relevance or facts. If you live in the Rearview Mirror, it's hard to listen, watch, leverage, and win!

Changeformational Prescription to Ensured Success

1. *As you reflect on what you just read, ask yourself whether you are living and evolving in the context of what you have read and, if so, whether you live in the context of a Change universe.*
2. *As you reflect on what you just read, ask yourself whether you are creating the new rules of business based upon the application of what you have just read and creating game-Changer realities for others to participate within. If so, you are Transformational!*
3. *Do you capitalize and leverage Change to place yourself in the lead; if so, you are **Changeformational!***
4. *Where do you focus: the Rearview Mirror, the Side Mirror, or the Windshield?*
5. *Adjust your time percentages to live in each according to the percentages above.*
6. *Stop, look, listen – The people around right now, these past 48 hours, where is their focus? That says a lot about where you are being pulled or pushed and that says a lot about where you are.*

Chapter Seven
The Disruption/Interruption Business Cycle™

Every decade for the past fifty years has had a massive global reboot occurrence. These shifts have created Change on every level of people's personal and professional lives. With it, many organizations have imploded, merged to survive, and struggled through the tough reboot; few have leveraged as **Changeformationalists** what others saw as Change and were able to accelerate to greatness.

Think about the last few Global Reboots:

1. 1990s – Dot-com companies experience uncontrolled growth and then the bubble implodes.
2. 2001 – 911 World Trade Center attack, impending Middle East Wars, and Civil Uprising "Springs"
3. 2008/10 – World Recession; Lehman Brothers and like businesses file for bankruptcy and the USA real estate market implodes.
4. 2020 – Chinese Corona Virus and the Global Pandemic Reboot
5. ? – What's the next big Change event?

Bringing the concept of Change stimulants or KPIs closer to where you live and work, consider what the Change inflection points are in life, business, and society and how people respond (logic-based), or react (emotion-based), to each.

Allow me to illustrate a way to look at the Changes in our lives and the Transformations you may need to undertake. In business, I call this the **Disruption/Interruption Business Cycle™**.

Below is a model I have adapted from Elisabeth Kubler-Ross's five stages of the Grief Cycle, and transformed into a life model as well as a business model.

First, recognize that most people (at least the 80-percenters from Chapter Five), just want to live and operate within the flat lines of either the left or right side. The flat line represents norms, routines and expectations; these are the KPIs that you live within. Once you know what is expected from you, (KPIs), then you associate the corresponding Tasks, Duties and Responsibilities (TDR) of an activity or a job, etc. to those KPIs. Next, draw upon or seek the Knowledge, Skills and Abilities (KSA) you must possess to survive and operate. In a job, you receive performance feedback or reviews along this flat line, as indicated by the first dot on the above bell-curve flat line.

The **Disruption/Interruption Business Cycle** then illustrates at the second dot on the flat line where a disruption or interruption may occur that causes a Change inflection point in your life. To understand when Change may appear or to even anticipate it, empowers you to be able to consider ways to expedite your time in the initial Change interruption left side of the curve that derails most people and organizations. The ability to reach the top of the bell-curve as efficiently, respectfully and quickly as possible, allows you to apply Transformational thinking to accelerate across the top of the curve and down the right side to **Changeformational** outcomes and new realities.

The derailer for most individuals and organizations is at that point (the dot) on the flat line where the interruption or disruption happens and the bell curve becomes an uphill challenge. When Change presents itself during your time on the flat line, you have been conditioned to waste time and invest a percentage of time at each point from the bottom of the curve to the top left.

The dot at the beginning of any upward curve is the **Disruption Interruption Point/DIP™**, and it can be constructive and positive or unforeseen, critical and negative.

When you can "anticipate" impending **DIPs** and position yourself and others to be prepared for them, you can leverage that dip for wins, and become **Changeformational**.

For most people and organizations, when they first encounter Change or especially shocking encounters, they immediately go into DENIAL. This then derails logical thinking and requires Change intervention and engagement endeavors – what a waste of time in the end.

Then, when this stage does not create the desired outcome, the next phase is spent attempting to avoid the new reality by exploding in ANGER – what a waste of time in the end.

Then, when ANGER does not create the desired outcome, the next phase is spent attempting to avoid the new reality by wanting to throw someone under the bus, as a deflection exercise in BLAME – what a waste of time in the end.

Transformation is about getting to ACCEPTANCE, as fast and prudently as possible, so energies can be focused upon OPTIONS and OWNERSHIP for **Changeformational** implementation and execution.

With ACCEPTANCE, comes a universal energy, a belief that we are all in this together. In essence, everyone has some degree, albeit differing degrees, of skin in the game. This collective buy-in takes place so you can let go of the left side of the bell curve and awaken to the vast opportunities of the right side of the bell curve.

With OPTIONS, your focus is solely upon leveraging where you are or any given change (the DOTs) and exploring Whitespace creativity and ideation of solutions towards not just transformation, but Changeformational outcomes.

The **Changeformational** leader or observer can recognize (anticipate, intuitively read, recognize, observe, assess), from within the flat line of the left side of the **Disruption/Interruption Business Cycle** what's on the horizon and, by Transformational action, institute systems, processes and procedures to minimize the impending Change stimulant, even avoid it in its entirety, while others are consumed by it!

The Transformational activities are aligned on the right side of the bell curve and flat line to bring everyone forward with a sense of confidence in what the future holds and what is expected from them.

Now, let's accelerate everything you just read. To take **Changeformational** to the next level, look at each of the past **DIPs** (whether negative or positive), as what you must have on your Dashboard. And even better is when you can forecast what the **DIPs** are. For example …

As the Trajectory Code V-Diagram above projects, there are what I call five levels of behavior that everyone will experience leaving Point A; there is no stopping the progression. The goal is to have insight and knowledge to always ensure that you are applying those behaviors in an AC Trajectory and, when you do so, you will always be in **Changeformational** Transformation mode. If you are not paying attention and consciously aware, those same five behaviors can actually propel you in an AB Trajectory, and Change will happen to you. You will be playing in others' games of life.

The five levels of Behavior.

As you leave Point A, we are all trained/educated in how to do what we do, I call this a Behavior (the conscious state or Level One). From here, as you see in the diagram on page 63 that evolves into a Habit (the unconscious state or Level 2). Over time we become so comfortable in what we do, how we do it, and why we do it the way we do that it now becomes a Personal SOP (Autopilot state or Level Three). Once you reach this state, with no accountability and feedback stimulus, we take Ownership (Personalized state or Level Four) of our actions. We now build a protective state around us and what we do. Our emotions play defense to any outside suggestions or questioning (Emotional state or Level Five). In the Trajectory Code V-Diagram AC-Trajectory application, this can have devastating consequences. Likewise, these same five levels of Behavior will actualize no matter what. Now if we arm ourselves consciously at each level, we can leverage this as Transformative in nature – every time.

Changeformational Prescription to Ensured Success

1. *As you reflect on what you just read, ask yourself whether you are living and evolving in the context of what you have read and, if so, whether you live in the context of a Change universe.*
2. *As you reflect on what you just read, ask yourself whether you are creating the new rules of business based upon the application of what you have just read and creating game-changer realities for others to participate within. If so, you are Transformational!*
3. *Do you capitalize and leverage Change to place yourself in the lead; if so, you are **Changeformational!***
4. *Do you forecast and lead others though disruption and interruption? Changeformational!*
5. *Do you look for others to lead you through disruption and interruption? Change rules you!*
6. *What can you do right now to take the lead in the next Change-cycle situation, and any future ones, to flow into Changeformational?*

Chapter Eight
S.T.O.P. - How to Make Decisions

"Analysis Paralysis" is considered by many to be significantly detrimental to entrepreneurial and business success today. However, for many individuals, the lack of meaningful accomplishment is not due to poor planning or application but, rather, an inability to make and execute educated decisions.

We live in a vibrant, ever-evolving world of Change. The decision-making process is a 360-degree lifecycle that loops endlessly. Learning how to make educated decisions quickly and effectively is necessary to keep up with the speed of today's business.

Three decades ago, I had the unique opportunity to study the decision process and make it user-friendly. I had been approached by IBM with a unique challenge – their sales teams and customer solution teams were getting caught up in the decision loop and losing client opportunities. They asked me to come up with a simple yet potent decision model.

I based my four-step decision loop model on the stop sign seen on roadways. Each letter directs you to one of the four essential decision steps and keeps you always moving forward. Since this formula was designed, it has been embraced and used by IBM to significantly increase the effectiveness of its planning, analysis, and implementation processes. Pfizer adopted the formula to increase team and sales effectiveness and to resolve selling-oriented conflicts. I have shared it with Boeing leadership attendees for years as a regular guest faculty member at the Boeing Leadership Institute. I also later shared this model in curriculum design work I did for seminar industry leaders' SkillPath Seminars and CareerTrack Seminars.

If you have an efficient process for evaluating, making, and executing decisions in real-time, fantastic! Keep doing what you're doing. However, if you see that your organization can get pulled into the weeds on even the simplest decision, allow me to share this powerful and **Changeformational** four-step decision model with you.

S.T.O.P.

The **S.T.O.P. Model™** allows you to facilitate a controlled and non-combative conversation through the four psychological steps of the decision-making process.

With this model, you can address procrastination; analysis paralysis; fear from impending failure within the decision process; and more importantly, inhibition of the execution or implementation actions of productivity needed today. You can ensure you work through any decision point, gather ample data and get appropriate subject-matter experts involved, as needed and when needed.

To facilitate Change and to accelerate Transformation, the four steps to the model and decision process are:

1. Step One: **S** - **Stop** and **See** what the stimulant is. Identify WHAT the situation or challenge is that needs to be addressed. Identify the WHAT factors to the conversation and decision issues. In essence, WHAT is the problem, situation, need, challenge, concern, opportunity, impending **DIP** or potential **DIP**, etc.?

   Once you have the core and legitimate subject-matter experts report on the stimulant, then everyone should be brought up to speed and know what they are there to discuss. You can now proceed. Ensure that you are not being distracted by noise or special interests, and not being directed to symptoms or ancillary issues.

2. Step Two: **T** - **Target** and **Think** through the reasons. WHY the "S" is worthy of conversation and explore the reasoning behind it, making sure you and everyone else understands the reasons for the topic, need, issue, challenge.

   This is the initial analytical step. Apply the **Player Capability Index™** to ensure that you draw upon the appropriate personalities/resources for their leveled insights. This formula walks you through the talent aspects of a person that can be effectively utilized to ensure the best talent around you is being sourced for making a decision. (The Managerial

Leadership Bible, graduate management textbook, and my Your Trajectory Code book detail this model). This is where the case for the "S" must be made and it is where you gain (or fail to gain), the buy-in of others. Then, after ample analysis and investigation, you can logically move forward to the third step. Ensure that all of the available subject-matter experts are engaged and their valuable input is gathered. Guard against hasty analysis and egos overrunning this step of the process.

In essence, make the case in your head or with others for why *this* issue, why are you dealing with it now. Does it even need to be addressed now? Why did it happen, or why was it missed?

This is the phase wherein you can deploy the analytics and deep thinkers, as necessary. You can utilize the business tools of SWOT, Gannt Charts, Mind Mapping, PERT Charts, DISC, and the lot ... just don't invest so much in this phase that you forget to move forward. This phase is fraught with analysis paralysis for many. Guard against this.

3. Step Three: **O - Organize Options** around HOW to address the "S." This is the innovation phase, the solution phase, and the go-forward phase. Here is where you want to hear and entertain multiple ideas from the people closest on the ground to the "S" and

the "T", and those who will have to implement the solutions.

Every discussion here should be an AC-Trajectory conversation. Use this step to generate multiple action plans; your first idea may not be the most viable, and you'll need other options to weigh against it. When you spend the majority of your time in this stage, it ensures greater final output and provides backup plans should your initial implementation plan implode. Again, ensure that all of the available subject-matter experts available are engaged and their valuable input is gathered so as to ensure powerful idea generation takes place. Guard against hasty forward momentum and egos overrunning this step of the process, as well.

Ask whether the solution being offered merely resolves the current situation or whether it can be used moving forward. Are the solutions merely more of how you would normally approach a problem, or are they Transformational in nature?

This phase is fraught with the fear of failure for many. You will need to guard against this. If you have viable options, then no matter what you select, you will always have a backup plan. You can proceed to the final decision stage with confidence.

Consider the markers of Change and those for Transformation discussed earlier in the book. Leverage this third step as often as possible to accelerate beyond just the decisions necessary to survive in the world of Change you find yourself in, and accelerate and elevate to Transformation.

4. Step Four: **P** - **Pick** the most viable option and **Proceed**. Here is the selection phase from the due diligence of step three. With viable solution "P", you have identified the WHAT to your next action and you have identified a timeline as to WHEN you are in the implementation mode of the solution. There should be very specific KPIs of WHAT you are to do or are doing so you will be able to track your forward progress.

As you evaluate your go-forward plan, ensure that you are leveraging this opportunity to be Better, Faster, Different, and more Cost Effective in what you do. This is what makes your actions **Changeformational**.

Once the fourth step is executed, it serves as a smooth loop back to letter "S;" then the sequence is continuously looped in real-time or as After-Action-Review metrics.

Once implementation is complete, reapply the **S.T.O.P. Model** to ensure continued success. Have check-in points throughout the four steps to ensure consistent forward progression and then do the same in the implementation phases. It is a learning process that will help you with all subsequent decision-making and implementation needs.

I worked with a CEO of a $4-billion company going through a merger. He and a senior leader were discussing bringing in a group of consultants to assist leadership with the merger. One of the individuals was advocating to hire a company featured on a podcast he had heard.

The CEO posed an observation to the group, "… while I am sure they are fine individuals, none of these people have merger experience; none have supervised a staff of employees or employees of our head count; and none have ever signed payroll checks for any size group, much less the size of our new combined organization." The CEO then asked the group, "Would it not make sense to hear from someone who actually has been through the merger process as a leader and who has actually had managerial responsibility and the experience of signing employees' checks?"

I walked him through the S.T.O.P. method in order to determine the ideal way to proceed. Armed with this tool, they decided against hiring the podcast company. They saved a lot of money and a big headache.

Using the **S.T.O.P. Model** to facilitate any decision is practical and accelerates your forward momentum in times of Change.

Using the **S.T.O.P. Model**, along with the other tools in this book, will drive you to become **Changeformational**.

STOP DECISION MODEL™

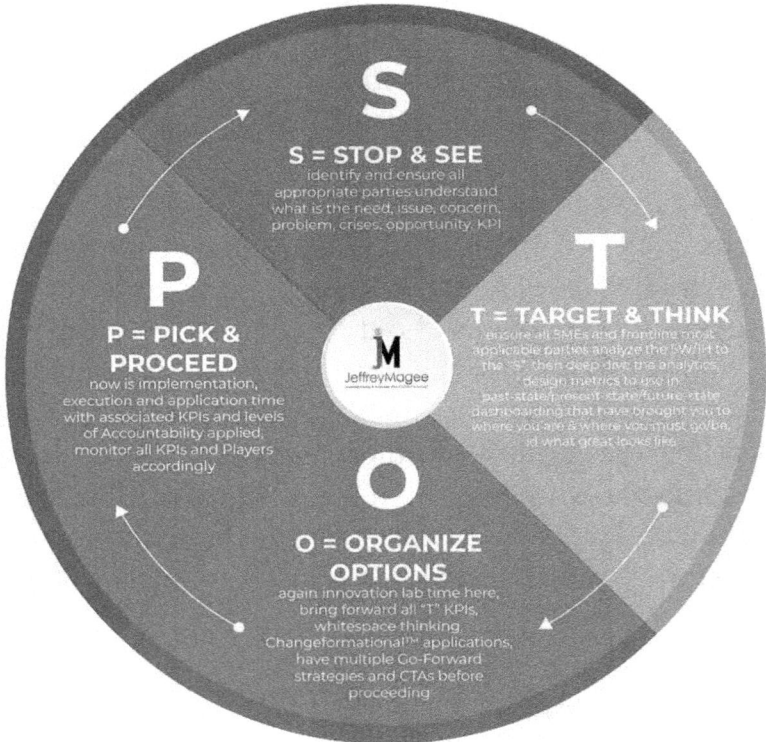

S = STOP & SEE
identify and ensure all appropriate parties understand what is the need, issue, concern, problem, crises, opportunity, KPI

T = TARGET & THINK
ensure all SMEs and frontline most applicable parties analyze the [W/H] to the "S", then deep dive the analytics, design metrics to use in past-state/present-state/future-state dashboarding that have brought you to where you are & where you must go/be, and what great looks like

O = ORGANIZE OPTIONS
again innovation lab time here, bring forward all "T" KPIs, whitespace thinking, Changeformational™ applications, have multiple Go-Forward strategies and CTAs before proceeding

P = PICK & PROCEED
now is implementation, execution and application time with associated KPIs and levels of Accountability applied, monitor all KPIs and Players accordingly

ReLoop STOP = Once you are in "P" mode ensure that you re-loop back through the model regularly to ensure effectiveness, success and desired ROI, this is an endless KPI loop

www.JeffreyMagee.com

JeffreyMagee

Now, let's accelerate the **S.T.O.P. Model** and the idea-generation/innovation stage of **"O"** and apply multiple previous models as overlays... The "O" is about Whitespace ideation off of your "S/T" being the Dot.

Run the individual go-forward strategies here through the question matrix presented earlier, and explore how your ideas can evolve from just being that of Change level to Transformative:

1. Better
2. Faster
3. Different
4. More Cost Effective

Here, you may generate additional last-minute discussions that could evolve your initial action plan forward and to a Transformational level. Look for ways to apply this four-step model to your new normal behavior and business operations so it becomes your new DNA: **Changeformational**.

By gaining macro insights and intelligence from your organization, industry, market, customers, supply chain, vendors, etc., you can evolve from the world of playing in the Change arena and living in and creating the Transformational arena that others will be attracted to. By dedicating a committed individual or team responsible to living these models and ideas within your organization, you will ensure strength today and relevance tomorrow.

In the next chapter, we'll discuss how to be **Changeformational** by applying these strategies and these models into your new life DNA and incorporating them into your organization on a continuous basis by holding yourself (and others), accountable.

Changeformational Prescription to Ensured Success

1. *As you reflect on what you just read, ask yourself whether you are living and evolving in the context of what you have read and, if so, whether you live in the context of a Change universe.*

2. *As you reflect on what you just read, ask yourself whether you are creating the new rules of business based upon the application of what you have just read and creating game-Changer realities for others to participate within. If so, you are Transformational!*

3. *Do you capitalize and leverage Change to place yourself in the lead; if so, you are* **Changeformational!**

1. *Do you make* **DIP** *awareness a part of your daily life?*

2. *Apply the* **S.T.O.P. Model** *to accelerate through the Windshield of Life opportunities.*

3. *Follow the insights of your* **FIST Factor** *to accelerate greatness.*

4. *Do you forecast and lead others though disruption and interruption?*

5. *Apply the Four Core* **S.T.O.P. Model** *into everything you do now; never accept okay!*

Chapter Nine
Accountability

Changeformational is a mindset; it is an action; it is a behavior; it is a way of being, knowing, and understanding. And it takes dedication.

In <u>The Managerial Leadership Bible,</u> a management textbook, I stated that individuals and organizations that experience high-performance achievement levels adhere to five strategic pillars or core characteristics. The last pillar or characteristic, Accountability, makes or breaks achievement. Without it, mediocrity becomes synonymous with accomplishment, and worse yet... it is rewarded.

Changeformational, at the end of the day, comes down to the execution of greatness. Beyond just staying in the game of Change and moving beyond writing the new rules of engagement as Transformational, it is the continued ability to leverage both Change and Transformation at any level, at any place in time, and with any individual you encounter – **Changeformational!**

You are responsible for being mindful of facts, informed of non-partisan research, and aware of differing opinions on any topic before forming a conclusion. Without this, you become susceptible to misinformation and bias. This practice is critical for Accountability to be a reality in an organization.

And thus, being **Changeformational** is married to Accountability.

The question we must address is whether we look at Accountability in a positive light, as a way to assist in the acceleration of greatness, or whether we see it negatively, as a signpost to resistance, deflection, blame, and derailment.

In working with the most accomplished Adjutant Generals of the National Guard, celebrities, athletes, politicians, Fortune 100 C-Suite leaders, and business owners and entrepreneurs of all levels, it is always the same – Accountability leads to sustained greatness.

If Accountability is not yet a part of your company culture, start small: incorporate this mindset into each of the following areas. This will lead to equality and sustained achievement.

1. **Job Description Accountability or Positional Description Accountability.** If you are doing 100 percent of your job description, you can consider yourself as 'meeting job expectations.' Job descriptions or performance expectations are critical, as each position is linked to an organization's overall output expectations. When accountability fails at an individual level, an organization is unable to produce and execute its marketed brand promise. It is the responsibility of

every individual to work towards the highest level of sustained performance output and to live up to your own brand integrity and that of any entity you are associated with. Accepting or fighting for anything less will lead to failure.

2. **Job Performance Evaluation Accountability.** Ideally, each performance expectation or KPI of a job description should correspond to an evaluation category on the performance review or assessment tool. These reviews can be measured and scored either by self-assessment (when honestly done), peer assessment, supervisory assessment, or organizational assessment. For example, if you are doing 100 percent of your job description, you can consider yourself as 'meeting job expectations.' To achieve an 'exceeds expectations,' you must exceed the KPIs of a job description. And the reverse is clear: for any job description KPI not attained, the score must be 'doesn't meet the expectations." This becomes an accurate feedback system for growth accountability!

3. **Personal Self-Accountability** is a more challenging reality today, based upon how your personal Dashboard of values, purpose, passion, and abilities has been calibrated. Your Dashboard KPIs from birth to your present age represent how you view

and embrace Accountability. This can differ based on: how you have been raised (generational perspective), education, culture, job experiences, personal associations, political and religious views, personal integrity instilled by elders (or lack thereof), etc. If you, yourself, have a high level of Accountability and hire individuals with this internal compass, then Accountability in your organization will be accepted and cultivated.

4. **Peer-to-Peer Accountability** is a natural outgrowth when peers understand one another, believe in one another and want to ensure that the best professional performance is taking place by one another. This is not an "I am going to tell on you" culture, it is an "I have your back and I don't want to let my peers down by not doing my very best every time" level of Accountability. Do you operate within a culture whereby everyone wants to win and everyone has one another's back?

5. **Organizational Accountability.** Do you walk your talk? Organizations with clear values and Mission Statements can benchmark every action, strategic decision, deliverable, and personal behavior. Accountability is not a game of Gotcha!, but an endeavor to do the right thing, at the right time, every time. Organizations are comprised of people,

so Accountability among people is essential to the organization. When organizations allow leaders to reinterpret Accountability standards, the erosion of achievement ensues.

6. **Laws-of-the-Land Accountability. Rules, Guidelines, and Laws** are set to maintain standards of expectations and excellence. To strive for greatness, raise the performance bar. However, once you make exceptions for one individual, you reset and recalibrate the performance bar downward. This derails entire institutions and entities that have been designed around the output of individuals to adhere to specific KPIs. Once this is done, it becomes an expectation by others, leading to conflicts within your organization.

7. **Cultural Accountability.** This is driven by an organization's values and vision and, once defined, it directs the corresponding output of its employees. How others describe you is a reflection of what your culture communicates.

8. **Time/Urgency Accountability.** Creating a work product consumes time. To ensure ROI to any output, consider the consumption of time as it relates to Immediate Time (level one), Intermediate

Time (level two), and Long-term Time (level three) as an implication for achievement.

9. **Trajectory Accountability.** When you begin to work on something, consider the trajectory of your actions. If you discover that it will take you towards constructive achievement, continue with greater commitment. However, if it would place you in a trajectory of failure or disingenuous output, you can recalibrate instantly and avoid wasted output and potential interpersonal conflicts.

In my book, Your Trajectory Code, available here (https://www.barnesandnoble.com/w/your-trajectory-code-jeffrey-magee/1121489916), I share pathways for achievement with three Accountability self-application questions:

(1) How can I apply this to myself/self-leadership?
(2) How can I apply this peer-to-peer with another/organizational/enterprise-wide application?
(3) How can I apply this within my organization/leadership/influencers?

10. **Institutional Accountability.** To truly ensure Accountability is a reality and that everyone is a super achiever, all KPIs should be elevated, and

Accountability expectations should be institutionalized. Peter Drucker asserted (and I agree), that 85 percent of what makes or breaks an organization is systems based, while 15 percent is people based. With turnover and the transitory nature of people (promotions, lateral and vertical movement, attrition, terminations, departures, downsizing, up-sizing, mergers, etc.), it is paramount that organizations identify those outputs and KPIs that are non-negotiable to their sustainment and growth. These must then become institutionalized (mandated by regulation, procedure, laws, etc.).

11. **Customer Accountability.** Consider your internal or external customers and ensure you have feedback loops for consistent, objective feedback (good or bad), that can be utilized in real-time.

Accountability allows for everyone, everywhere, every time to participate and execute their expected and appropriate level of participation. Without Accountability, someone always has to achieve more to cover for those who produce less. When you allow Accountability to slide, you penalize those who perform and reward those who learn how to take advantage of others. In the end, everyone loses. On the other hand, achievement through accountable behaviors, conduct, and psychology grows integrity in individuals and drives an organization to succeed. Even more importantly, it fosters a **Changeformational** Mindset.

In order to guide my clients (and you, the reader), to a **Changeformational** way of being, I've simplified this system and identified 5 Accountability levels you can work through.

1. Self-Accountability, Level One

   Starts with you willing to hold yourself up to the highest level of performance and the fullest display of your DNA capabilities, and the same for any enterprise you lead. If you and those around you could freely, unconsciously operate at this level, the need for Accountability levels 2-5 would not be necessary. Few live in Transformation, because most fail at level one.

2. System-Accountability, Level Two

   To ensure you operate at level one, create compliance-style Accountability, mechanisms, dashboards, cohorts, and feedback loops to ensure that the expectations, guidelines, rules of engagement, laws, etc., that you must live within to exist as the environment was intended. The System creates Accountability and ensures everyone plays by the rules and that no sub-entity or non-constituent dictates the rules.

It is as simple as driving a car down the road: you know that a red light means stop and a green light means go, and when this is not followed as the system dictates, problems ensue.

3. Peer-Accountability, Level Three
   Creating relationships and environments wherein colleagues have each other's backs and step in to help and ensure no one degenerates the expectations. And, when people know, appreciate and enjoy those they live with, work with or associate with, then Transformational realities occur. People raise the performance bar on one another and help others to see through their Windshield to greatness – **Changeformational**.

4. Customer-Accountability, Level Four
   How do you engage, solicit feedback from and act upon the experiences of those you serve? Do you have a relationship or system that allows for a free, easy flow of data from the customer to the closest touchpoint with the customer and senior levels?

5. Boss-Accountability, Level Five
   Everyone has skin in the game. How connected are leaders, owners, core stakeholders? While it is obvious they should, and must be, connected, the

point of level five is that they come into play last. If level five must be present for levels 1-4 to deliver, you will never be Transformational. You will never be at the top of the list, Thriving in times of Change. You will exist, but you will always be in Change modes or survival.

The reason we see so much abdication of personal responsibility is that we are either missing or unwilling to adhere to level two.

To overcome Change and be Transformational, we must be held accountable to perform.

You can embrace Change initiatives, leverage talent and resources for Transformational ability and become comfortable as **Changeformational** individuals, teams and organizations. However, when you make an exception to Accountability, you will backslide. When you make an exception or allow for less-than-expected performance, you are actually ensuring low performance. If an individual or organization cannot sustain Changes of culture, systems, processes, or procedures, then what you have done to be Transformational will merely become the norm. Everyone else will Change to be relevant, and then everyone will be, once again, on an even playing field.

To be **Changeformational**, everyone must not just accept but embrace, anticipate and champion Change as the minimal expectation in their life. Everyone must be adept at spotting opportunities to Transform how they think and what they do. The energy and spirit of Transformation must become a daily mantra and **Changeformational** behaviors must be held accountable.

Changeformational Prescription to Ensured Success

1. *As you reflect on what you just read, ask yourself whether you are living and evolving in the context of what you have read and, if so, whether you live in the context of a Change universe.*

2. *As you reflect on what you just read, ask yourself whether you are creating the new rules of business based upon the application of what you have just read and creating game-Changer realities for others to participate within. If so, you are Transformational!*

3. *Do you capitalize and leverage Change to place yourself in the lead; if so, you are **Changeformational!***

4. *What percentage of time is spent at Accountability levels 3-5 to ensure success? The higher the percentage of time and resources deployed here, versus Accountability levels one and two, the less likely you are to reach **Changeformational** status.*

Chapter Ten
Core Expectations

Changeformational is about aligning a lot of variables. I have always observed that the most overlooked variables are the human capital variables. When you have those aligned, it is amazing how individuals and organizations can continuously Thrive at the level of **Changeformational**.

Stop and reflect for a moment on possible people you have observed around you or stories you've heard about living examples of **Changeformational**. Perhaps you have read about someone or a business, or you are a customer of a **Changeformational** business. Or perhaps you know someone... or you are the someone, who has changed their life trajectory of late. They are no longer doing what they used to do, but are now doing something that aligns with their values and purpose. It allows them to really draw upon their knowledge, skills and abilities (talent), and what they are doing drives and feeds their passion – **Changeformational**.

Years ago, within my own businesses and when consulting with others, I began to realize that there are three core Expectations in any organization. These three are seen and interpreted by the organization and the individual.

And, when I sat on the side of the desk of the organization or employer, I recognized that the same three Expectations employers have are the same as those held by the employee.

What I recognized by listening to employers was that when they have rock-star employees, it was because the employee and employer aligned in these three areas. And conversely, when an employer and employee were sideways with one another, it was also because of an issue in one, or a combination of, the same three areas. Employees and employers love or hate organizations because of these reasons.

They are:
1. Job/Position
2. Organization
3. Personal/Boss/Employee

For example:
1. I love my job and what I do.... I hate that organization; the job I was hired to do is not what they have me doing!
2. I love the organization and what I do.... but I hate my Boss!

3. I love my Boss and what I do … but I hate the organization; they are not living up to what I was told they would do!

This idea can be applied to the interviewing and onboarding process, the performance review discussions, and ultimately, in how promotions, advancements, and job opportunities occur. This will reflect on how aggressive or passive your Performance Development Plans look. Use this list as a powerful KPI list in performance check-in discussions. And, when faced with a Change situation, consider where it lies within these three Expectation areas and what is most likely going to be impacted. Then have a **Changeformational** discussion at that level.

> When all three Expectations are aligned (between employee and employer), then everyone is operating at peak performance. It creates the perfect environment for everyone to be **Changeformational!** When these three areas are not aligned, you regress back to merely surviving. Work gets missed or executed at a minimal performance level. Passive-aggressive behaviors appear, and tensions, anxiety, and stress increase.
>
> This creates tension points or **DIPs** that can lead to the implosion of the relationship. Now no one is

Transformational and everyone is merely looking to find ways to Change to survive. And when this is not possible, implosion begins.

Visualize it this way ...

ORGANIZATION	INDIVIDUAL
1. Positional	1. Positional
2. Organizational	2. Organizational
3. Personal	3. Personal

First, share from the organization's perspective the Expectations of the person to occupy the position, then ask the potential new employee whether they understand said Expectations. Then, ask the potential new hire or potential promotable person what their Expectations of the position are. Ensure that you are all aligned.

You would have this same two-way conversation about the Expectations of the organization and personal Expectations. Here is what the organization expects out of or from everyone. Here are the personal Expectations that you have. And what are the employees'?

There are many ways to calibrate alignment on these three Expectation forces, and thus, ways to ensure you are always aligned for Transformations to naturally take place:

1. Values – Are the values of each party in alignment? If either party is not 100 percent aligned, one party will feel as if they are making a concession, and concessions are never sustainable in the long term.

2. Mutual Understanding & Agreement – All parties must ensure open, clear, concise communication before and during any endeavor or relationship to ensure that, if any factor on any of the three Expectations are to Change, at any time, are all parties in alignment with that Change?

3. Goals – What are the immediate, intermediate and long-term goals of each party in relationship to each Expectation, and are these documented and or understood before and during the relationship's journey?

4. Associations – Ensuring that the associations, causes and philanthropy that you engage in or support are aligned with one another.

Positivity grows Changeformation in everyone and everything you do. Normalcy and complacency will lead to decay, negativity will raise its head, and you will find yourself back at survival mode!

To evolve and operate at the level of **Changeformational**, all of the human capital must be more often aligned than not.

Changeformational Prescription to Ensured Success

1. *As you reflect on what you just read, ask yourself whether you are living and evolving in the context of what you have read and, if so, whether you live in the context of a Change universe.*
2. *As you reflect on what you just read, ask yourself whether you are creating the new rules of business based upon the application of what you have just read and creating game-Changer realities for others to participate within. If so, you are Transformational!*
3. *Do you capitalize and leverage Change to place yourself in the lead; if so, you are* ***Changeformational!***
4. *Are you in alignment?*

Section Three
Changeformation in Action

The days of business, whereby an individual or organization could slowly evolve and slowly make changes in what it did or delivered, are gone. Consumers and employees want new and evolved deliverables and experiences; people are not willing to wait for "someday" to arrive. They want it yesterday.

Being truly **Changeformational** requires relevance. Relevance is what draws people to you and why you exist. It is that factor that others cannot quite attain, and thus, allows you to Thrive in a marketplace with many others merely competing and surviving. In the next chapter, we will discuss what relevance looks like for your business.

Chapter Eleven
Radical Relevance™

To ensure you and your business are always at the ready and do not become complacent, the concept of **Radical Relevance** must be baked into your organizational DNA, in every strategic business unit and with every leader. While many major businesses globally have engaged R&D teams or departments that can execute **Radical-Relevance** exercises, most businesses do not have the size, scope, or resources dedicated to ensuring they are Transformational.

Strategically, the concept of **Radical Relevance** works off of five "RE" Factors or word sets, and tactically, how you execute each could be limitless. In my executive and leadership work, I train a series of strategic and tactical KPIs or ways to facilitate each. This is how you regularly test, challenge and explore areas of Change potential and opportunities to be Transformational. At every level of your organization, you should run the **Radical-Relevance** exercise on your:

1. Strategy (macro and Strategic Business Unit micros)
2. Values
3. Vision

4. Operational Systems
5. Processes
6. Activities
7. Procedures
8. Behaviors
9. Core deliverables

Decades ago, I worked with the financial services industry running a Certified Professional Education (CPE) certification firm and working with the top CPA firms and professionals across America. I learned of an exercise called a financial stress test. This is where you explore, push, and plan for best-case and worse-case scenarios to ensure the financial stability of your organization. And it can be adopted, adapted, and applied for **Radical Relevance** across all business lines.

Being **Changeformational** is all about **Radical Relevance**, and the five stages to Radical Relevancy is the exercise you should challenge your senior leaders to do within their work areas and with their junior leaders, SMEs and teams on a regular basis (at least monthly).

Factor One – RE-EXAMINE:
Apply the simplicity of the 5W1H Model, the S.T.O.P. Model or any other analytic optics you know and like to everything in your work area; Reexamine

- WHAT you do
- WHY you do it or do it that way
- WHO does it or calls the shots
- WHEN you do it
- HOW it is done
- WHERE it is done
- WHAT is going right
- WHAT are the challenges

You can utilize this matrix in a number of situations:

1. Everything is going great. It's time to challenge yourself and others to run the **Radical-Relevance** model against everyone and everything being done to protect against complacency and to consider opportunities to Change up, step up, level up, and create more efficiencies, effectiveness, and thus, profitability.

2. A situational challenge or problem has arisen. It's time to challenge yourself and others to run the **Radical-Relevance** model.

3. You are considering a new process, product line(s), merger and/or acquisition, inviting in a new capital player, physical plant expansions or new locations,

hiring new talent, creating new positions/roles into your organizational chart, etc. It's time to challenge yourself and others to run the **Radical-Relevance** model.

Factor Two – RE-IMAGINE:

With the clarity of the identified item from factor one, the Re-Imagine step is about innovation, creativity, and/or the validation that what you are doing is the best that can be determined. The power of this exercise and this specific step being undertaken on a regular basis, is that it does provide you with potentially Better, Faster, Different and or more Cost-Effective KPIs and ways to proceed. You may unearth forward-focused Change opportunities in doing this, and you may accelerate beyond yesterday by revealing, at this step, ways to Transform who you are, what you do and how others will be made to change to keep up with you.

This step and overall exercise done on a regular basis may just save you and your organization from an AB Trajectory, or being manipulated into others' wins and your ultimate loss!

This second step, or **Radical-Relevance** factor, allows for a person or organization to always be cutting edge, as this exercise could be couched, "if we were starting this business today, what would it look like, feel like and how would it operate? What would it be doing that we are doing now and what would it not be doing that we are doing now?"

Factor Three – RE-BRAND:

Whether the output from the second exercise or factor is a renewed yes to the Re-Examine and Re-Imagine or it reveals a new output, the universe associated with you needs to be reaffirmed and Re-Branded with the new you!

Look at what the organization says, projects, and affirms inwardly and ensure that is what is being perceived from the outside.

Factor Four – RE-ENGAGE:

Now it is time to evaluate and engage all of the appropriate constituents and ensure everything being done matters and everyone doing it is operating at peak performance.

Have the right talent in the right place at the right time. They must be resourced, supported, guided, and compensated appropriately to ensure that all the appropriate communication channels and streams are working at peak performance. It is paramount that everyone is engaged. If someone is not, manage that person or deliverable out of the organization as fast as possible. Set the cadence for success and set the conditions for achievement.

Ensure that you have feedback loops from all parties inside and outside, as appropriate, to ensure that what you have Re-Examined, run through the Re-Imagine loop, and selected as the Re-Brand is, in fact, being Re-Engaged as expected.

Factor Five – RELEVANT:
Want to ensure that you are relevant and not just believing your own public relations? Then consistently run the **Radical-Relevance** exercise at the executive (ownership) level of your organization and push it throughout so every key leader and business unit regularly allows themselves time and permission to challenge everything they do. This needs to become institutionalized and a part of your organizational culture to ensure you never find yourself waking up one day and realizing the market passed you by and you are forced into survival mode of a world that has changed.

Being **Changeformational** makes you and your organization relevant. Otherwise, you will live a life of Change that may be disastrous for you. Now you have been mentally equipped to adapt, adopt, improvise, forecast, envision, and grow in a constantly Transforming world to become innovatively **Changeformational!**

When you know what your brand identity is and you know what works (why you are relevant), then double down on this secret ingredient(s) and leverage yourself forward.

To ensure you and your organization are Radically Relevant, and that you live a greater percentage of your time in the **Changeformational** action space and less in Change, ensure you have the stimulation and resources for that reality. Here are a few KPIs to accelerate that:

1. Ensure your **FIST Factor** is always evolving and pushing you forward …
2. Apply the Trajectory Code V-Diagram to everything in your life to ensure you are on an AC Trajectory and leveraging every 1-Percent factor opportunity.
3. Create Transformational management groups/teams within your organizations. These can be specific individuals you pull together for a specific mission or for Transformation on a larger scale. Make sure it always has a few outside subject-matter experts, the appropriate internal subject-matter experts, and includes the final user/customer into the design and implementation feedback loops.

4. Ensure you have more Transformational markers to your name and fewer Change markers, as described early on in this book.
5. Make sure you are always blending your dot and white-space DNA.

Then you will be **Changeformational** in Action and **Radical Relevance** will become your new comfort space!

Changeformational Prescription to Ensured Success

1. *As you reflect on what you just read, ask yourself whether you are living and evolving in the context of what you have read and, if so, whether you live in the context of a Change universe.*

2. *As you reflect on what you just read, ask yourself whether you are creating the new rules of business based upon the application of what you have just read and creating game-Changer realities for others to participate within. If so, you are Transformational!*

3. *Do you capitalize and leverage Change to place yourself in the lead; if so, you are* **Changeformational!**

4. *What aspect of your business is most critical to your viability? Run the five stages of the* **Radical-Relevance** *model now in your head to find out.*

5. *Which player in your business is most critical to your viability? Run the five stages of the* **Radical Relevance** *model on them now in your head.*

6. *What strategic business unit of your business is most critical to your viability? Run the five stages of the* **Radical Relevance** *model on it now in your head.*

7. *What would happen if you tasked 100% of your critical leaders to perform this drill on their respective areas and provide an operational situational brief to all of their fellow senior leaders in ten days? Run the five stages of the* **Radical-Relevance** *model on it now in your head.*

Conclusion

Change is evolutionary and happens. Transformations will occur, with or without you. **Changeformational** is how you ensure you always WIN!

Changeformational is when you instinctually are always evolving internally and externally, setting new levels of execution, performance, and excellence. It is when you change how customers engage with you and others at such a level that it simultaneously attracts new demographics and changes how service, culture, mind-shifts, business, manufacturing, and/or distribution does what it does ... That's where the true game changer lives and radiates outward from as you are writing the new rules of engagement and business.

Changeformational is when you look outside your **FIST Factor** of connections and search out new influencers to surround yourself with and invite into your mental space to challenge you to greater levels. It may be when you seek out a coach for self-improvement or an advisor for business and professional improvement. But here is the deal maker: vet the credentials of those you seek counsel from. One experiment I do is to check people out on LinkedIn, the world's #1 online professional business platform, with more than one billion users. Look at their

LinkedIn profile and really review their work experience, credentials, certifications, education, etc. When I need a quick humor fix I do this, as about 90% of the time, the person putting themselves out there to help you has "NO CREDENTIALS" on their profile. They may also show constant job turnover, that they are licensed/certified in everyone else's intellectual property

- Content
- Programs
- Services
- Deliverables

and yet, none of their own. While perhaps they are great self-marketers, they are out of their depth! A **Changeformational** implosion in the making.

I once saw a person designated by an online entity as the #1 Business Coach/Consultant globally. A quick review of their LinkedIn profile and website supported no such claim. They had never been published in that space; the number one conference in the world on their topic (where I had the honor of being the opening or closing Keynote Speaker for two decades), had never heard of them; and the #1 author/consultant in that space for the past 30 years, who writes for me regularly in my publication www.ProfessionalPerformanceMagazine.com, had never heard of them. So, buyer beware.

To calibrate yourself toward more **Changeformational** opportunities and wins, ensure you have the right real-time **FIST Factor**. Recognize if your tendency is to be a dot- or white-space personality. Either one is great, and it's the ability to merge the two together that creates **Changeformational** opportunities.

Recognize from your past life if the traits of Change are where you live now or are the traits of Transformation more comfortable to you?

I have built my life around being **Changeformational** with integrity, purpose and passion. I have designed my business to leverage my entirety of life experience to serve others through our Leadership Master Class series and my Sales Master Class series, which truly allows the individual to grow, achieve and win!

The global clients I work with, from personal one-on-one advisory/coaching at an elite level to the engaged organizational C-Suite leadership work, is all built upon values, purpose, and long-term vision that allows for a unique sustained relationship – magic happens, and phenomenal results are created.

Give yourself permission to understand and align yourself with opportunities, people, and places that feed your

Expectations in life. Embrace the difference involved in the decisions we and others make in the world of Change and Transformation. Always manage your ego. Never allow ego to manage you. Then you will always be **Changeformational!**

Change ensures that you will SURVIVE.
Transformation ensures you will THRIVE.
Changeformation ensures you WIN!

If you'd like to know more about how we can work together in a **Changeformational** manner, visit www.JeffreyMagee.com and learn more about my programs:

1. Dr. Jeffrey Magee | Leadership Mastery
2. Dr. Jeffrey Magee | Performance Driven Selling
3. Dr. Jeffrey Magee | Coaching & Consulting

About the Author

Dr. Jeffrey Magee, for more than 30 years, has served as a C-Suite Executive and Professional Publisher/Editor-in-Chief of www.ProfessionalPerformanceMagazine.com. He is the Best-Selling Author of more than 31 books translated into 21 languages, including 4 best-selling graduate management textbooks. Dr. Magee works with Business Owners, C-Suite Leaders, global business CEO-to-CEO networks (like VISTAGE & YPO), and Military Generals to significantly increase their organizational effectiveness through progressive, innovative Human Capital talent development training, initiatives, coaching, and senior level Advisory work!

He has designed the core curriculum of **THE LEADERSHIP INSTITUTE: The Leadership Academy of Excellence Series/1.0-3.0.** It should be noted that in the past 5 years, 100% of Jeff's clients, ranging from $500M to $6B in annual revenue, have posted their best revenue years in business, year-to-year!

Jeff is a

- **CMC -** Certified Management Consultant
- **CBE -** Certified Board Executive
- **CSP -** Certified Speaking Professional
- **PDM -** Certified Professional Direct Marketer

In his speaking engagements, he has shared insights and ideas globally with professionals in more than 30 countries and across the USA in 52 states/territories!

Connect with and learn more about Jeff at:

www.JeffreyMagee.com

www.ProfessionalPerformanceMagazine.com

(99+) Dr. Jeffrey Magee, CMC/CBE/PDM/CSP | LinkedIn

A Whitespace Doodle Page
(for Someone Special)

www.ingramcontent.com/pod-product-compliance
Lightning Source LLC
Chambersburg PA
CBHW050502190326
41458CB00005B/1398